D1358337

THE WORLD OF
BLUES

Groveton High School Library
38 State St.
Groveton, NH 03582

Groveton High School Library
38 State St.
Groveton, NH 03582

THE WORLD OF
BLUES

David Harrison
Foreword by B B King

THE
Aristocrat
OF RECORDS

U-7148

YOU'RE GONNA' MISS ME
(When I'm Dead and Gone)
(Muddy Waters)
MUDDY WATERS
with
Rythm Accompaniment
1307A

MANUFACTURED BY THE ARISTOCRAT RECORD CORPORATION CHICAGO, ILL.

CHARTWELL
BOOKS, INC.

ACKNOWLEDGEMENTS

*For Becky,
Corin and Laura,
with love*

With thanks to B B King for providing the foreword; Ian A Anderson (editor, *Folk Roots* magazine); Cilla Huggins of *Juke Blues* magazine for reading and correcting the proofs; Tony Burke of *Blues & Rhythm* magazine; Dave Peabody, photographer extraordinaire; Johnny Parth and Hannes Folterbauer for permission to use cover images from the Wolf Record and Document blues labels; Dave Foster, Hot Shot Records, Leeds; Ken Smith, Red Lick Records, Porthmadog, Wales; Adam Sieff at Tower Records, Piccadilly, London; John R T Davies for supplying the majority of the 78s record labels; Richard Wootton; photographers Terry Cryer and Tim Motion. In particular, much gratitude to the handful of devoted researchers and collectors who lovingly preserved the fragile 78s and found and interviewed the musicians before it was too late. Without their belief in the importance of the music, our knowledge of the blues would have been too fragmentary to even consider a book like this.

Courtesy *Juke Blues* (copyright as cited below)
Chris Strachwitz/Arhoolie Records, 2, 3, 8, 94 (below left), 120 (above left), 135 (above right); 3; 7; André Hobus, 10 (above), 106 (below), 133 (above); 12 (below); Peter Amft/Alligator Records, 14 (above left), 104 (below left), 138 (below right); Mick Huggins, 15 (below), 103 (below); Brian Smith, 16 (below left); Cilla Huggins, 32, 87 (below left), 104 (below right), 108 (below), 109 (above right), 109 (below), 110, 111 (below left), 128 (above left); 47; 53 (above left); Axel Küstner, 58 (above left), 67 (below); 63 (above left); Paul Harris, 65 (above); G. W. Proper, 66; 67 (above left); 71 (above); 77; 83 (below); 88 (below); 88 (above right); House of Sounds, 89 (above left); Brian Baumgartner, 89 (above right), 115 (above left); 90 (below left); 91 (below right); Volker Albold, 91 (above); Brian Blauser, 91 (below left); 92 (above right); 92 (below left); 92 (below right); 93 (above left); Johnny Otis/Jonas Bernholm, 93 (below); 94 (above right); 94 (below right); Eddie Shuler, 94 (above left); 95 (above left); 95 (above right); 97 (below right); 97 (above); Jerry Haussler/Solid Smoke Records, 98 (below left); 99 (below left); Brian Smith, 99 (above); 101 (above right); 102 (below right); 102 (below left); Gerard Doidy, 103 (above); Lasse Lindedal, 104 (above), 129 (above left); Big Bear Records, 105 (above); 105 (below); 106 (above right); Pete Welding, 106 (above left); Ray Flerlage/Delmark Records, 107 (above left), 119 (above left); Marc de Jonghe/Robert Vanderschueren, 107 (below), 121 (below) 127 (below), 128 (above right), 132 (above right); Gerard Robs, 108 (above); 110 (inset); 111 (below right); Brian Smith, 112 (above); 115 (above right); 115 (below right); 116; Tano Ro, 117 (above left); Denis Lewis, 117 (below left), 117 (below right); John Taylor, 118; 119 (above right); Hiram Dotson, 120 (below); 122 (above right); 123 (above); 123 (below right); 124; 125 (inset); John Perriss, 126 (above right), 130 (centre right); 127 (above left); 128 (below right), 129 (below right); Brian Smith, 129 (above right); Jan Loveland, 130 (below); Robert Tilling, 130 (above); Kirk West/Alligator Records, 131 (above left); Demon Records, 131 (below right); Brian Smith, 132 (below); Irene Young, 132 (centre left); Pierre Degeneffe, 134 (below); Paul Natkin, 135 (above left), 135 (below left); Denis Lewis, 137 (below left); David Crossan, 138 (below left); 139.

© **Tim Motion:** 6

© **Dave Peabody:** 10 (below right), 53 (right), 68 (above), 70 (below), 79 (above left), 79 (below), 100, 114 (above), 126 (above left), 126 (below), 127 (above right), 127 (centre right), 128 (below left), 130 (above right), 131 (above right), 133 (below), 134 (above right), 135 (below right), 136 (below left), 137 (above left), 137 (above right), 138 (above right), 139 (below).

Courtesy *Blues & Rhythm* (copyright as cited below)
Kim Komenich, 11 (above left); Sylvia Pitcher, 27 (below

left); 37 (above right); G. P. G. M. van Rijn, 41 (above); 43 (above right); 45 (right); Henry De Lorval Green, 64 (above left); 72; 75 (above right); 79 (above right); 80; 81 (right); 83 (above); 87 (below right); 89 (below right); 90 (below right); 95 (below left); Brian Smith, 102 (above), 114 (below left), 119 (below); Ingemo and Charley Nilsson, 111 (above), 134; Jacques Grimbok, 113; 115 (below left); 115 (above left); 117 (above right); 121 (above left); Roland Stuckey, 123 (below left); Paul Harris, 132 (above left), 136 (below); 136 (above right); 137 (below right); Paul Natkin, 138 (above left); Brian Smith, 139 (above right).

© **Terry Cryer:** 13; 74 (below right); 112 (below right).

© **Redferns** (also copyright as below)
Max Jones Collection, 51 (above left); 113 (below).

©**London Features International Ltd/Michael Ochs Collections:** 18, 22, 25 (right), 26 (left), 30, 42 (left), 44, 46, 48, 60, 71 (below), 76, 81 (left), 82, 84, 90 (above), 92 (above left), 96 (above), 96 (below), 97 (below left), 98 (above), 99 (below right).

© **1993 John R T Davies:** 24, 25 (left), 26 (right), 27 (centre right), 28, 29, 33, 34, 36 (right), 50 (right), 51 (above left), 51 (below), 52 (right), 53 (below left), 54, 57, 59, 86.

© **Document Records:** 17, 35, 39, 45 (left), 52 (left), 64 (right), 65 (below), 67 (above right), 69 (right), 74 (above), 78.

© **Burt Goldblatt/Sony:** 78

© **United States Information Service:** 20

JACKET CREDITS
Front panel, large, © Dave Peabody; above small, © André Hobus/courtesy *Juke Blues*; middle small, © David Redfern/Redferns; below small, courtesy *Blues & Rhythm*. Back panel, courtesy *Juke Blues*.

PUBLISHER'S NOTE
Every effort has been made to locate and credit copyright holders of material reproduced in this book. The publishers apologise for any omissions. These will be corrected in any future editions.

Published by
CHARTWELL BOOKS, INC.
A Division of **BOOK SALES, INC.**
110 Enterprise Avenue
Secaucus, New Jersey 07094

Copyright © Studio Editions Ltd, 1993

Design by Ann Samuel

All rights reserved. No part of this publication may be reproduced, stored in a retrieval system, or transmitted, in any form or by any means, electronic, mechanical, photocopying, recording or otherwise, without the prior permission in writing of the copyright holder.

ISBN 1 55521 935 7 (hardback)

Printed and bound in Singapore

Mance Lipscomb (page two), a Texas songster discovered in the sixties and whose repertoire ranged far beyond the blues. An unrivalled repository of old ballads and pre-blues songs.

Contents

Foreword

The blues have been around now for nearly a century and they are still alive and kicking. It is the music of my people, the black residents of America, but it speaks to the world.

The blues came out of the plantations of the Deep South, the travelling shows, the bars and speakeasies. And as black people moved to the big cities of the north and west, the blues followed them and changed to reflect life on the streets as they had reflected life in the country.

Blues speaks *from* the heart and soul of the people *to* the heart and soul of the people. Blues is more than just music – it's a feeling, and I know from my travels around the world that the blues can move and inspire anyone, from Russia, Israel, Africa and Europe, to Japan, Asia and Australia. Music is a common language and the blues is an important part of that language.

But it is a changing language. My own music has developed a lot since I started back in the forties, but it's still

the blues. And it's good to see young players like Robert Cray, Joe Louis Walker, Jeff Healey, Kenny Neal, Eric Clapton and Buddy Guy building on the foundation stones we laid, and keeping the music growing.

You'll find the blues at the heart of most modern pop music, from jazz and funk to rock to soul. No other folk music has been so influential or had so many thriving children. Yet even today there are young people interested in going back to the roots of modern music and learning about how the blues began, about the singers who developed the many different styles of the blues and about the way the music had changed to match the times. And that's what this book is all about.

From Charley Patton and Blind Lemon Jefferson, through Muddy Waters and Howlin' Wolf, to the young lions of today runs an unbroken line of musicians who each helped forge another link in the chain. I am proud to be among them and delighted I have been able to introduce the blues to so many people in so many countries.

B. B. King

Introduction

The blues? According to singer Georgia White, 'They ain't nothin' but a woman cryin' for her man'. Robert Johnson complained they were 'a low-down achin' heart disease' and 'a shakin' chill'. Blind Lemon Jefferson saw them in Texas 'loping like a mule', while Buddy Guy met tham 'walking through the woods'.

The blues have come a long way since they were sired by poverty and deprivation in the poor black areas of the American Deep South. The music has been cleaned up, prettified, abused, ignored, abandoned and rediscovered. And even today, 70 years after the first blues were recorded, you can still find blacks in America who sing in a way that their grandparents would recognize.

Perhaps the durability of the blues is due to the basic simplicity of the music. But then it isn't simple music. The heart of it may be a 12-bar song with an AAB lyric structure, but that is a small part of the story. The blues

Lightnin' Hopkins, 'the most creative folk poet of our time' according to Arhoolie Records boss Chris Strachwitz. He recorded hundreds of sides, including many enduring classics, and even an instant tribute to the first man on the moon.

can be romanticized as the cry of a people in chains, but blues music is also entertainment. There are bitter songs about racism, poverty and unfaithful lovers, but plenty of others which are simply good-time dance numbers or amiable, bawdy jokes.

Not every song with Blues in the title is truly the blues. Not every black singer is a blues singer. And not every blues singer sang just blues. What we call blues is just one facet of a rich tradition of black music which developed, largely in the Southern states of the USA, in the years after the Civil War (1861–65).

To the millions of immigrants it attracted, the USA must have seemed like the promised land – huge expanses of wide open spaces, rich soil, uncountable natural resources. People went there from all over Europe and later Asia, looking for a new life away from ancient feuds and the nationalist hatreds which had kept the Old World continuously at war for centuries. These immigrants took with them their traditions – and their music.

The new American folk music grew from Scottish and English ballads, Irish jigs and reels, German polkas, waltzes and two-steps, French accordion traditions,

All that remains of the birthplace of major blues star Muddy Waters on Stovall's Plantation, Mississippi.

The circle closes. Mali musician Ali Farka Toure (right) is a great fan of John Lee Hooker whose intense rhythmic style is much loved in Africa.

Mr Lucky. John Lee Hooker, once a mainstay of the Detroit club scene and now an international superstar who has rock stars queueing up to play with him.

Spanish rhythms and, of course, African music. With the settlers came slaves, torn from their homes, shipped across the Atlantic in truly appalling conditions, and sold with brutal disregard for family ties. Was there anywhere in the world where so much varied music fought for a hearing, where there were so many influences and so many styles all jostling for attention? The new musics that came out of this extraordinary melting pot had a large number of stepparents, and they inherited the best of all of them.

Jazz, ragtime, minstrel melodies, vaudeville popular song, the uniquely American orchestral composers like Louis Gottschalk, Scott Joplin and Charles Ives – would any of them have been possible in anything but a new country determined to create a culture which might borrow from the old but which transformed those influences into something new and exciting?

No one really knows how the blues developed, or when, but it seems likely that it was in the early years of the 20th century. Musicologists have discovered links between some African music and the blues, mainly in the use of African scales, the famous blue notes (flattened or bent notes), and in its very melodic outline. There was also a strong tradition in Africa of guitar- or banjo-style instruments (probably introduced by the Portuguese in the 15th century), and blues historian Sam Charters suggests a credible link between early blues accompaniments and West African finger-picking styles.

There's a pleasing feeling of the circle being completed in contemporary Mali musician Ali Farka Toure, who is strongly influenced by John Lee Hooker, a bluesman whose intensely rhythmic style strikes a common chord with African listeners. It's a link which fascinates Ry Cooder, a white American guitarist whose own records are heavily influenced by the roots music of his country; hillbilly, Cajun, Tex-Mex, blues, old European dances and rock 'n' roll are blended by Cooder into a kaleidoscopic swirl of musical colours.

In a revealing interview in the British *Folk Roots* magazine, Cooder said Mali musicians regarded Hooker as 'some kind of messenger ... a presence beyond being a blues guy. He plays irregularly, his bar count is funny, he doesn't change the chords in a normal sort of triad way, and they don't either. So they see something familiar in that. Ali Farka Toure plays that way. He really is a mirror image of Hooker. He's like the backward version.'

Cooder has an ambition to have the two men play together to see if the link is more real than perceived. 'I want to see if it's true that what we call the blues, just because it's been called that for some crazy reason, is really this spherical, global thing that it probably is.'

Sadly, no one thought of doing anything like that in the early days of black music in America. But it does seem that what we call the blues dates back only to the turn of the century as a specifically defined music, although the use of the word 'blue' to describe a doleful or gloomy mood is centuries old. The blues song – usually the first two lines repeated and a third to round off the verse – undoubtedly existed before it was documented, but as a part of the rich heritage of black music that covered ballads, spirituals, minstrel songs, ragtime, country dance bands, work songs, field hollers and even European dances like the waltz.

Several revealing accounts survive of life on plantations in the 19th century. Religion (Christianity) was encouraged – loyalty to the master on earth meant riches in heaven – although white Christians often disapproved of the way that blacks introduced movement and rhythm into their services. But many white people loved the sound of the Negro spirituals, possibly because they owed more to European hymns than African music, but also because of the rich harmonies and an overall sadness, a sense of yearning for higher things. What they didn't appreciate is that many of the spirituals had alternative sets of words expressing a desire for freedom and justice on earth, as well as in the next world. Most early recordings of Negro spirituals were aimed at white audiences, but some very authentic performances were issued by the Dinwiddie Colored Quartet in 1902, and one dim, scarcely audible cylinder recording

Fred McDowell, last of the truly great Mississippi bluesmen. Discovered in middle age in the late fifties, he made a superb series of recordings of traditional Delta blues which feature some of the best slide playing ever recorded.

of the Standard Quartette has survived miraculously from 1894. (Note the variant spellings of quartet/quartette at this time.)

More fascinating relics of the 19th century were recorded in 1909 by Polk Miller, a former Confederate soldier, unrepentant apologist for slavery, and banjo player, with the Old South Quartette, a group of blacks with whom he toured widely. The records include the Rebel army anthem, 'The Bonnie Blue Flag', with the quartette providing loud hurrahs in the chorus. What they must have thought about that can be imagined. But apart from two spirituals, the Quartette also sang a laughing song, serenaded 'Oysters And Wine At 2 am', and imitated cats and dogs. Mark Twain, who heard them perform, called them 'the only thing the country can furnish that is originally and utterly American'.

The Old South Quartette's recordings are possibly the best surviving examples of authentic nigger minstrel music (nigger has always been an offensive term, but the word appeared in many blues recorded in the 1920s). But in an interview in 1892, Miller gave an intriguing insight into Southern attitudes towards black music. The spelling and condescending mock dialect is as printed.

I was raised on a plantation where niggers were thicker than hops and it was there I learned to pick on de ole banjo. I wouldn't tell nobody that I even knowed how to play the banjo because it was looked upon as a nigger insterment and beneath the notice of the cultivated ... I do play the nigger banjer and now and then as I pass along the road I delight in getting behind a Negro cabin and singing a plantation melody jes' to see 'em come a crallin' out to see who is dat out dar a-playin' on dat banjer.

Miller's repertoire included white hymns, but also Negro spirituals and popular plantation songs like 'Go Tell All the Coons I'm Gone', 'Gwine Back to Dixie', 'Carry Me Back to Old Virginny' and 'Swannee River'. His scrapbooks contain a unique documentary of black folk banjo styles, which dated back to at least 1830.

They were one influence on the blues, probably heard at its finest in the 1927 recordings of Banjo Joe (Gus Cannon, leader of one of Memphis's best jug bands). Cannon was born in 1883 and his six Banjo Joe sides include 'Poor Boy Long Ways from Home', one of the earliest of all documented blues, together with ragtime pieces and minstrel or sardonic medicine show songs like 'Can You Blame the Colored Man'. Even more intrigu-

Jesse Fuller, a highly popular one man band from Georgia, whose songbag included country dances, gospel, blues, ballads and even music hall.

ingly, 'Poor Boy' is the only recorded example of a banjo played with a slide (in this case a knife was used to stroke the strings). Was this unique to Cannon, or was he simply the only one to get slide banjo on record?

Another important ingredient in the blues was the work song and the field holler, or arhoolie. Work songs were rhythmic call-and-answer songs used to help keep time on jobs which needed coordinated team work. There are plenty of examples of these on record, and the work song lasted long after the blues came to dominate black folk music. The ballad of 'John Henry', recorded memorably by Furry Lewis in Memphis, John Hurt in Mississippi and Georgian Jesse Fuller among many others, started as a work song. And Howling Wolf, one of the greatest of the Mississippi bluesmen, told Pete

Kenny Neal, son of Raful, and a highly acclaimed recruit to the ranks of classy Louisiana singer-guitarists. His albums are particularly thoughtful and well balanced.

Welding in *down beat* in 1967 of the work songs he heard in his childhood.

> *Some of the fellows was making songs like 'I worked Old Maude and I Worked Old Bell' – things like that. They'd just get out there and sing as they worked. Ploughing songs, songs to call mules by. They'd get out there mornings and get to ploughing and get to hollering and singing. They'd make these songs up as they go along. They'd make their sound and their music just like they feel. They made up the works songs as they felt.*

One work song contained the line, 'I got the blues but I'm too damned mean to cry.' Wolf would have heard a combination of work songs and field hollers. These were sometimes little more than musical shouts made by gangs when the line shouted by one man would be picked up and passed on by others, sometimes just an 'are you there' call from one lone worker to another in a distant field. Huddie Ledbetter, better known as Leadbelly, recorded a number of hollers and work songs, including

'Whoa Back Buck', 'Julia Ann Johnson' and 'Line 'Em', and there was a very unexpected throwback in the form of a track lining song by the otherwise unknown Bootney on a 1988 record by young Louisiana blues singer Kenny Neal.

Work songs, spirituals, ballads shared between black and white performers, minstrel and travelling patent medicine show songs all contributed to the development of the blues. What no one knows is when blues first developed and where.

Historian Sam Charters believes it was in Mississippi. But, as British researcher Paul Oliver points out, blues were sung and played across an enormous area of the Southern United States, and in communities far removed from each other by distance, climate and social conditions – the equivalent of a folk music which flourished simultaneously in Copenhagen, London, Rome and Cairo.

Many blues singers from the first generation recalled in later years that they had never heard of blues when they were growing up. They knew the music as rags, reels, or just dance music, and their repertoire would contain far more than just 12-bar songs. These days, black singers who recorded more than blues are sometimes called songsters to distinguish them from the straight blues singer. It's an artificial distinction, imposed by the limitations of knowing the music solely from recordings. Who knows what Jim Thompkins played apart from the one beautiful slide guitar-accompanied blues that is his sole recorded legacy? Charley Patton, the most revered of all the heavy-voiced Mississippi singers, was better known among his contemporaries as a clown addicted to Jimi Hendrix-style guitar antics. Isaiah Nettles, the 'Mississippi Moaner', was noted for tap-dancing while he played. Even Robert Johnson, possibly the most influential blues singer of all, including 'Yes Sir, That's My Baby', 'My Blue Heaven' and 'Tumbling Tumbleweed' in his shows.

But the meagre evidence available suggests that the blues emerged as a separate, definable music around the turn of the 20th century. The most interesting account of the new music came from W. C. Handy, a bandleader and composer who in 1903 heard 'a ragged, lean Negro guitarist' at a railway station in Mississippi. 'As he played, he pressed a knife on the strings of the guitar in a manner popularized by Hawaiian guitarists who used steel bars. The effect was unforgettable.'

The song contained the line, 'Goin' where the Southern cross the Dog', a reference to the junction of the

Southern Railroad and the Yazoo-Delta (Yellow Dog) Railroad in Mississippi. Handy remembered it and later included it in his own 'Yellow Dog Blues'. His conversion continued at a dance date, where he allowed a local group to play a spot while his own, strait-laced band had a break. There was a guitarist, mandolin player and bass player, and Handy described the music as 'over-and-over strains that seem to have no beginning and certainly no ending at all. The strumming maintained a disturbing monotony but on and on it went, a kind of stuff which has long been associated with cane rows and levee camps.' He was staggered when the crowd went wild and the three boys collected more money than the Handy orchestra was getting for the evening. 'Then I saw the beauty of primitive music', Handy commented drily.

He went on to orchestrate many blues tunes he picked up on his travels, and although he was never a blues performer in the real sense, he certainly brought the music to the attention of the public. In 1912 he publised 'Memphis Blues' and it could be argued that the formal definition of the blues dated from that time.

Most people think of blues songs as having a simple AAB structure; certainly, that is the form which underlines blues in the jazz sense. But the great blues singers, the ones who added something unique to the music, often wandered from 12-bar, and there are wide variations in structure and form. It's possible that the two repeated lines followed by a concluding third may have developed to allow singers time to think up that third line, but a music which depends on improvisation can never be too bound by rules. Consequently, even as late as 1927, Big Boy Cleveland could record an archaic 'Going to Leave You Blues' which repeated each line three times (his other record was a solo on the ancient quills or pan-pipes, which also suggests he was a veteran performer). Georgia street singer Peg Leg Howell's haunting 'Skin Game Blues' has even less of a 12-bar structure, with a four-line narrative verse and three repeats of the last line with interjections, before an ABA chorus.

Whether the blues came from Mississippi or not, there is no doubt that the state produced a large number of the finest and most intense blues singers, from Charley Patton and Son House through to Muddy Waters and Howling Wolf. That's no surprise if you take the romantic view that the blues is a cry for help from an oppressed people.

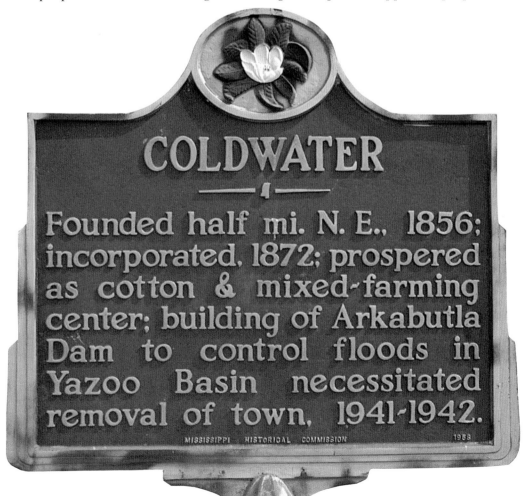

Coldwater, Mississippi, one of the many northern Mississippi communities famous for its blues artists.

By the end of the 19th century, there was a greater concentration of blacks in Mississippi than any other state, especially in the so-called Delta between the Mississippi and Yazoo rivers. This was rich land, given over largely to cotton and needing cheap labour. White dominance was absolute, with harsh segregation laws, brutal economic slavery, appalling mob lynchings and a repression which, even in the 1960s, was compared to Nazi Germany. Blacks were herded into their own communities and developed their own lifestyle based on the church and ramshackle bars and dance halls. Thousands of black families fled to the North, taking the blues up-river to Memphis and then to Chicago and Detroit.

The Delta blues echoed the rhythmic emphasis of the work song: the vocals were heavy, coarse and unrelenting, with falsetto used for contrast or emphasis, and

Reverend Gary Davis, a blind street corner preacher who also recorded blues and country dance tunes. One of

the finest guitarists on record and a fierce singer who was, luckily, widely recorded.

slide guitar often adding a second voice. It's easy to say that Delta blues reflected the anguish of life for blacks in a state from which a third of the black population moved in the 10 years to 1960, but that's too simplistic. It was a combination of many factors, including, perhaps, less of the influence by white music which made the blues of the East Coast states much lighter and more melodic. But social conditions must have had some effect on the intensity of the music.

Slide guitar was just one form of blues playing; another equally attractive variation used a raggy dance rhythm, fingerpicked with astonishing dexterity in the case of masters like Blind Blake, Willie Walker, William Moore and Gary Davis. But there is something particularly haunting about slide guitar, especially on a slow, moody blues where it can be used in duet with the voice, or to complete unsung vocal lines. And even within this one form of blues playing, there are numerous variations and stylistic effects.

The slide itself can be a knife, a small bottle, or a bottleneck or brass tube fixed on one of the fretting fingers. The guitar can be played in the normal upright position or laid across the lap, Hawaiian-style, like the Georgian Kokomo Arnold, Texan Black Ace, or Oscar Woods, the Lone Wolf, from Louisiana. The slide can be used on one string to give a shrill, whining sound like a violin, or chordally to generate a hollow, ethereal moan. A very few players, like the highly gifted Blind Willie McTell, used it with a bulky 12-string guitar to create a lonely, windswept sound evocative of a train whistle or a distant riverboat.

The idea of sliding an object across the strings may have come from the Hawaiians, as W. C. Handy suggested, although one theory is that slides were used to imitate the sound of the fiddle, which was a popular instrument in Negro bands of the last century. Folklorist Howard Odums wrote about slide guitar in 1911 as knife songs, a method by which skilled performers could make a guitar talk and sing.

One of the songs he mentioned as played with a knife was 'Poor Boy, Long Ways from Home', which Banjo Joe recorded on that unique knife-played banjo in Memphis in 1927, a few months after Georgia singer Barbecue Bob recorded it using a bottleneck on a 12-string guitar, and a year before Rambling Thomas from Texas put out his own variation, again with slide. It's not surprising with such a widespread song that Alan Lomax and Shirley Collins taped one of the best of all recorded versions from John

ISHMAN BRACEY
& CHARLEY TAYLOR

1928—1929

Complete Recorded Works
In Chronological Order

document
RECORDS

DOCD-5049

Ishmon Bracey, a dour
colleague of Tommy Johnson
who abandoned the blues to
become a minister.

Dudley at the notorious Parchman Farm Penitentiary in Mississippi as late as 1959.

Not all blues have guitar accompaniment, of course. There is a vast and very rewarding tradition of piano blues, ranging from simple underpinning of vocals and jolly dance tunes to complex music imitating the guitarists and offering improvisations of considerable skill and beauty. A trawl through the standard discographies will find blues accompanied by kazoo, ukulele, tiple, harmonica, organs, jugs, accordion, standard orchestra reeds and brass, whistles, fiddles, vibraphone, xylophone, jazz bands of various sizes, washboards and even home-made instruments.

But the blues with its emphasis on sex, drink, unfaithful lovers, violence and wandering found little favour among strict church-goers, who regarded it as the devil's music. It was little wonder that people like Son House were torn between the blues and the church, or that some believed that Robert Johnson, the archetype of the fast-living, womanizing blues singer, must have sold his soul to the devil in exchange for his skills.

Georgia Tom, who churned out some fine blues and bawdy hokum songs such as the amazingly popular 'Its Tight Like That', finally caved in, abandoned the devil's music and became Professor Thomas A. Dorsey, much-loved and respected writer of some of the most popular gospel songs of the century. Others managed to bridge the gap, but had to change their names on record; Delta bluesman Charley Patton became Elder J. J. Hadley for two religious sides, Blind Lemon Jefferson masqueraded as Deacon L. J. Bates for his religious numbers, and Blind Boy Fuller and his colleagues became Brother George's Sanctified Singers. Guitarist John Byrd was converted to the Reverend George Jones; Kansas Joe McCoy surfaced for a while as Hallelujah Joe; his one-time wife Memphis Minnie cut two tracks as Gospel Minnie, while Mississippi singers Reuben Lacey and Ishmon Bracey turned to the ministry in later years and rejected the blues altogether.

It worked the other way, too. Guitar evangelist Blind Joe Taggart made a blues record under the pseudonym Blind Joe Amos, and it is believed that the unissued sides by Blind Texas Marlin hide the secular work of the great gospel singer Blind Willie Johnson. The Reverend Gary Davis lost the chance of making more than a handful of records pre-war when he refused to play blues (he relented in later years to give some idea of what was missed), and there are many other examples of the great divide.

For some it never really mattered. Blind Willie McTell sang anything from blues and gospel to the odd bit of hillbilly under various names, although he turned increasingly to religious music in his later years.

Two intriguing views of the argument came from members of the Five Blind Boys of Alabama, a highly respected gospel group since 1939: 'I love blues singers like Bo Diddley, Jackie Wilson, Roy Hamilton', said Clarence Fountain in an interview with Ben Sandmel. 'And remember now, blues folk always steal things from gospel. But I don't think the blues is evil, it just depends on the spirit. Ninety per cent of blues singers is Christian people just out there making money anyway.'

Colleague George Scott started playing guitar after hearing a record by Blind Boy Fuller, but he had a traditionalist church-going father who wouldn't let him play 'reels' ('he called 'em reels, that's an old timey word'). When he was caught singing 'My Baby's Gone and She Won't Be Back No More', his father appeared unexpectedly, asked drily, 'How far did she go, son?' and then whipped him. Scott remained philosophical. 'The difference is on our side we say "Jesus" and the blues singers, they say "baby".'

1
Goin' Up the Country

The Beginnings

T he first blues to be recorded were a very long way from the field hollers, or the song of that ragged, lean Negro W. C. Handy heard in Mississippi. In fact, few of the first 'blues' on record bore any more relationship to the music than the titles.

Yet it was the recording of the blues that changed the music irrevocably. Once the music became easily available in shops or by mail order, it became difficult to trace the originator of a popular song, or to be certain whether the earliest version on record *was* the original or simply the result of one singer getting a recording date before another.

Many songs copyrighted by performers or record company executives were traditional verses, allegedly arranged by the copywriter, or, as in Handy's case, orchestrated from folk tunes. Medicine show entertainer Jim Jackson had a giant hit with 'Jim Jackson's Kansas

Ma Rainey, the Mother of the Blues, and a wonderful soulful singer. Despite the poor quality of her recordings, Ma's songs did much to alert northern record companies to the marketable sounds of the south.

Jelly Roll Morton is best known for his marvellous New Orleans jazz recordings, but he was also a deeply moving blues singer and excellent pianist.

City Blues', for instance, yet Robert Wilkins, a brilliant and unusually melodic blues singer, claimed to have composed it, and the Memphis Jug Band recorded their own version in the same month in 1927 as Jackson.

Georgia Tom Dorsey, one of the few bluesman wise enough to register his compositions, admitted that before blues were recorded there was usually a kind of communal ownership of blues music. 'Blues was blues. All blues belong to you.' He added, 'All blues sounded alike for a while anyway, so we never bothered about the other fellow. If he got something of yours out, that's OK. I'd just let him take me out to dinner or something like that. And if he thought I'd infringed on him, there was never any money transaction. We used to say, "Who can rhyme music?" We would say, "I'm gonna play something and you put words to it." I would compose right as I go along. Some of those guys could do pretty good.'

Jelly Roll Morton, self-styled inventor of jazz, was also a deeply moving blues singer, as his solo recordings from the late 1930s show. He was a great one for claiming to have composed songs to which his claim was dubi-

ous, to say the least, but his memories of the early days of New Orleans are priceless. He was there in the early days of jazz, which succeeded ragtime, a syncopated music derived from banjo rhythms to which serious composers like Scott Joplin brought an elegant, timeless beauty. New Orleans in Morton's youth was a musical melting pot, with marches, formal French quadrilles, blues, and Morton's famous Spanish tinge emerging from the cauldron as jazz.

Perhaps boogie woogie, a heavy, very rhythmic kind of piano blues, started here as well. Rudy Blesh, the chronicler of ragtime, quotes New Orleans resident Roy Carew in a famous description of boogie as the 'little bad boy of the rag family who wouldn't study'. There were certainly blues there as early as the turn of the century, if Morton's memory is to be trusted. He made several recordings of the wistful 'Mamie Desdoumes' Blues', the first blues he ever heard, which he claimed was in 1902. Mamie Desdoumes was a neighbour who had lost two fingers on her right hand and knew only this one tune. Morton also recalled for the Library of

Congress a blues player called Game Kid. 'He was as ragged as a pet pig. He just played that piano all day long after he'd get up and he'd go around from one girl's house to another – what they call the goodtime houses – not for any financial purpose at all, just to have a lot of fun.' One of Game Kid's numbers, which Morton recorded for the Library of Congress, was 'Honky Tonk Blues No. 1'.

And there was Buddy Carter, 'a man who could really play those blues and those things we call stomps today'. Morton made several recordings of 'Winin' Boy' (mostly cleaned up from the bawdy original), which he claimed was 'one of my first tunes in the blues line down in New Orleans', and 'Michigan Water Blues', a speciality of legendary New Orleans pianist Tony Jackson.

Another of Morton's Library of Congress recordings was 'If I Was Whiskey and You Was a Duck', which appeared in W. C. Handy's version of 'Hesitating Blues' and as 'If the River Was Whiskey and I Was a Diving Duck', transferred into blues by numerous singers from Sleepy John Estes through to Muddy Waters. Morton claimed to have written a song he recorded variously as 'Alabama Bound' and 'Don't You Leave Me Here', but this was a classic example of a traditional song being hijacked. It is thought to date back to the 19th century, although it was first published as 'Alabama Bound' in 1909, four years after Morton said he wrote it. It was certainly very popular; Texan Henry Thomas, possibly the oldest black singer recorded, waxed two slightly different versions ('Don't You Leave Me Here' and 'Don't Ease Me In'), Papa Harvey Hull turned out a fine 'Don't You Leave Me Here', and Papa Charlie Jackson, a highly popular entertainer of the 1920s, offered 'Alabama Bound' as early as 1925.

Jelly Roll Morton's memories of New Orleans were collected in 1938, and were no doubt embroidered by time, but New Orleans was obviously a major source for the earliest blues. Yet surprisingly, when the big record companies started recording on location, 25 years after the golden years Morton recalled, they found few major blues artists, and most of those they did record there were brought to the city from elsewhere. The most interesting session from a strictly New Orleans point of view was by the Victor company in early 1927, when they concentrated on first-class jazz, but also picked up Richard Rabbit Brown, a boatman with a speech disorder, who recorded one superb blues, two delightful minstrel show songs and two long and detailed ballads. Sadly, he

never recorded again, unless it was him masquerading as Blind Willie Harris at a 1929 Vocalion session in New Orleans, as some collectors believe. But the 1927 session also captured the light-voiced Genevieve Davis singing with Louis Dumaine's marvellous Jazzola Eight, and the formidable Ann Cook, a woman with a grim reputation, who seems to have repented in the 1950s and joined the church. But apart from minor artists like Esther Bigeou, Lizzie Miles and Willie Jackson, New Orleans remained a low-key blues city until the post-war years.

But the lively city that Jelly Roll Morton remembered, and bluesmen like Tony Jackson and Game Kid, live only on paper, as do legends like jazzman Buddy Bolden, who was supposed to have been the best. Who can tell? No one was interested in recording them and they remain little more than faded memories. Black jazz of a sort was recorded before 1920, although it was largely stiff and formal rag-based music, like the endearing sides cut by James Reese Europe's Hellfighters. But no one in the early record industry bothered with selling to the 14 million American blacks – an unknown market just waiting to be tapped. Many, of course, still lived in rural communities down South. Others were beginning to seek a new life in cities like Atlanta, Memphis and Chicago. In fact, between 1910 and 1920 the number of blacks living in a small area of Chicago rose from 44,100 to 109,600.

A theatre for black audiences had been opened in the city as early as 1905 and offered 'ragtime, cakewalks and coon songs', the black equivalent of the white music hall or vaudeville. Many musicians had moved into the city, some from the New Orleans red-light jazz area of Storyville, which had been closed down by the Navy because of the number of fights involving sailors. Others were veterans of the travelling entertainment industry – circuses, minstrel shows (there was a curious market for blacks blacked up and acting out white stereotypes of Negroes) and medicine shows. The latter featured patent medicine salesmen who used entertainers to attract audiences. Many early blues singers played with the medicine shows, including Gus Cannon, Furry Lewis, Jim Jackson, Speckled Red and even the alcoholic and highly influential Tommy Johnson.

Chicago, the natural target for migrating blacks up from the South, rivalled New York in the opportunities it offered. Louis Armstrong and King Oliver headed there, as did numerous blues singers like Georgia Tom. Pianists found ready employment in wine rooms (rooms in the back of bars where women were allowed to drink), rent parties (literally parties to raise money for rent) and buffet flats (high-class brothels and out-of-hours drinking establishments).

Dorsey recalls he was popular because he played and sang softly, so the police wouldn't be alerted. His music, already a bit dated compared with the new jazz, also struck a chord with the immigrants from the South. Jazz, explained Dorsey, was 'peppy'. Blues was 'feeling bad ... ain't got no whole lot of pep to jump around like the jazz'. Popular dances of the time were the shimmy and the slow drag, and Georgia Tom's music was just right. As he recalled in an interview in 1977:

> *Blues were not played or sung in high-class places or in smart society clubs. They were heard in the black and tan joints, the smoky little hole-in-the-wall joints, broken-down road houses and second-rate vaudeville houses.*
>
> *Blues would sound better late at night when the lights were low, so low you couldn't recognize a person 10 feet away, when the smoke was so thick you could put a hand full of it in your pocket. The joint might smell liked tired sweat, bootleg booze, Piedmont cigarettes and Hoyttes Cologne.*

Blacks in the big cities were homesick for the kind of music they had left behind in the South, a point not lost on Perry Bradford, a vaudeville pianist, songwriter and bandleader based in New York. More sophisticated blacks, who had made a new life for themselves, ostensibly despised the blues as working class, an unwelcome memory of an oppressive system from which they had been lucky to escape. But Bradford still believed there was money in blues, and in 1918 put together a blues revue called *Made in Harlem*. It played to packed houses.

He had also been trying to get record companies interested in making records for the black communities (particularly of his own songs), but without success. This wasn't surprising; even when he managed to press Fred Hagar of Okeh Records to take a chance, Hagar received threatening letters from white pressure groups warning him that Okeh products would be boycotted if he recorded coloured singers. Hagar stuck to his guns, and on 14 February 1920 Mamie Smith, a rather limited black cabaret singer, recorded two of Bradford's pop songs with a white band. The record sold 10,000 copies in a month.

Perry Bradford wrote in his autobiography: 'God bless Mr Hagar, for despite the many threats, it took a man with plenty of nerve and guts to buck those powerful groups and make the historical decision which echoed round the world.'

Mamie Smith returned to the studio that August to make a much more important record, 'Crazy Blues' (another Bradford song) with her Jazz Hounds, a scratch band including cornettist Johnny Dunn, and possibly Willie the Lion Smith on piano. It might not have been the real blues, but it was a staggering success, selling 75,000 copies in the first month. And it opened the floodgates.

'Crazy Blues' was hardly a great record. It had been written in 1912 under the original title of 'Nervous Blues', but it was what it stood for that was more important than the actual music. It set Mamie Smith on the road to stardom; she went on to make nearly 100 records and was able to ask $1,500 a week on tours. Ironically, her records, like so many of her contemporaries', are usually prized more these days for the fine jazz accompani-

Georgia Tom Dorsey (left), singer, pianist, and co-creator of the hokum hit 'It's Tight Like That', who gave up the blues to write some of the best loved gospel songs. A revered figure in both blues and church circles.

Lucille Hegamin (right), one of the more successful cabaret blues performers of the twenties, with her Blue Flame Syncopators.

ment than for her singing, although contemporary accounts and memories from other singers like Victoria Spivey suggest that she was better live than on record. She led an expensive life of fast cars and luxury homes with a string of lovers, but the Depression ended the big spending. Mamie Smith tried to make a comeback in 1940 with a number of short films, but her day was over. She died in poverty in 1946, almost completely forgotten.

She was followed on record in November 1920 by Lucille Hegamin, 'the South's favourite – a cyclonic exponent of darktown melodies', who came from Georgia and was nicknamed the 'Georgia Peach' (not to be con-

fused with gospel singer Clara Gholston Brock, who recorded in 1942 as Georgia Peach).

Hegamin was another light-voiced, pop-orientated singer, but record buyers loved her. She claimed in later years to have been the first to sing Tony Jackson's 'Pretty Baby', to have popularized Handy's 'St Louis Blues' in Chicago, and to have been presented with the original manuscript of Jelly Roll Morton's 'Jelly Roll Blues' when she worked with him. Her biggest hit was 'Arkansas Blues', and she toured widely with her Blue Flame Syncopators.

Numerous other women singers with a largely thea-

trical or club background were recorded in the early 1920s as record companies realized there was a totally new market out there. They eventually became known as Classic blues singers, although the blues content in most of their records was very thin.

But by 1922 there were enough well-known names to hold a blues singing competition in New York at which Lucille Hegamin, Trixie Smith, Daisy Martin and Alice Carter took part. Trixie Smith (no relation to any of the other blues-singing Smiths) won with 'Trixie's Blues', but she is best known today for a blistering session in 1925 backed by Louis Armstrong as part of Fletcher Henderson's Orchestra, and a pleasant 1938 set which did more for Sidney Bechet's reputation than hers.

A few names stood out from the crowd churning out endless jazz and pop songs with blues in the title. There was Rosa Henderson, a sweet-voiced singer with a very endearing style, whose accompanists were the cream of the jazzmen. There was Ida Cox, 'the uncrowned queen of the blues' and a skilled composer, who sang more real blues than most; Ethel Waters, who soon abandoned the blues for stage shows and films; and Victoria Spivey, an astringent singer but fine songwriter, who set up her own record label in the 1960s to record the surviving Classic blues singers (and many others).

Victoria Spivey was a highly regarded Classic blues singer and songwriter who started her own record label in the blues revival. She had several singing sisters, including Addie 'Sweet Pease' Spivey, and Elton Spivey Harris, the 'Za Zu Girl'.

Sippie Wallace (right), who recorded with Louis Armstrong in the twenties and with Bonnie Raitt in the seventies.

PRICE 75c
TRADE MARK REGISTERED

Paramount

12049-B   Blues

You Can't Do What My
Last Man Did
(J. A. Johnson and Allie Moore)
Alberta Hunter
Acc. by Thomas Waller
1456

Alberta Hunter made some pleasant jazz-blues records with Fats Waller, Louis Armstrong and other top jazz stars of the twenties, and recorded with some of the survivors in 1961.

Among the more popular women singers were Clara Smith ('Queen of the Moaners'), the sentimental Eva Taylor, piping-voiced Alberta Hunter, jazzy Edith Wilson, Edmonia Henderson, Margaret Johnson and Viola McCoy. Very few have stood the test of time – possibly a reaction to the years when collectors looked on blues as little more than the roots of jazz. However, it's instructive that the largest reissue of Classic blues in the CD era has been a boxed set billed under the name of Louis Armstrong – originally just part of the accompaniment.

Many of the women singers like Ida Cox, who made records in the early days of the Classic blues boom, had gained experience in the touring tent shows of the South, which took varied entertainment to rural communities. One of the finest was Cleo Gibson, part of a husband and wife team called Gibson and Gibson, who made two magnificent sides ('Nothing but the Blues' and the sexual boast, 'I've Got Ford Movements in My Hips'), which were almost the equal of Bessie Smith at her best.

Perhaps too similar, for Gibson tragically never recorded again and nothing more is known of her.

Other singers popular in the South included Lillian Glinn from Texas, who was even serenaded in a blues by Atlanta singer Barbecue Bob; the tough-voiced Bertha Chippie Hill, who made a first-class series of records with accompaniments as different as Louis Armstrong, Georgia Tom and Scrapper Blackwell; the warmer-toned Sippie Wallace from Texas (who recorded with rock singer Bonnie Raitt in her later years), and her sister Hociel Thomas; and Lottie Beaman or Kimbrough, the 'Kansas City Butterball', a rich and resonant vocalist.

Many of these women sang on the TOBA circuit – a chain of theatres willing to stage black acts, although

not noted for its generosity. The initials stood for Theater Owners' Booking Agency, but the artists reckoned it meant Tough on Black Asses. Apart from the blues singers, the TOBA circuit booked jugglers, snake-charmers, comedians – anything audiences wanted to see.

Among the most popular acts were husband and wife teams, swapping insults and singing blues-based songs. The best known were Butterbeans and Susie, Coot Grant and Kid Wesley Wilson, and George Williams and Bessie Brown. All recorded extensively, but the forced humour has dated horribly and, again, their records are sought today more for the accompanists than the headline artists.

Out of this huge outpouring of jazz, vaudeville and dreary pop, two names stand head and shoulders above the rest, and both are still avidly listened to for their own sakes, as well as the backing groups: Gertrude Ma Rainey, 'Mother of the Blues', and the incomparable Bessie Smith.

It is one of the great tragedies of the blues that Ma Rainey recorded only for Paramount, a company not noted for its devotion to high fidelity. Even the cleanest 78s give only the barest hint of her majestic voice and extraordinary power and presence. She was a real blues singer, and one of the very finest. She offered the sounds of the South and audiences adored her showbiz flair, her wonderful sense of staging and, above all, her expressive singing. Georgia Tom Dorsey, who played in her backing group, knew little about the blues when he first heard her in Georgia in his teens, and wasn't sure he liked what he heard. But in an interview in the late

1970s he painted a wonderful picture of Ma in her prime when he was in her band.

She stands out high in front with a glorious bust, squeezed tightly in the middle. Her torso, extending in the distance behind, goes about its business from there on down. When she started singing, the gold in her teeth would sparkle. She was in the spotlight. She possessed her listeners; they swayed, they rocked, they moaned and groaned as they felt the blues with her. A woman swooned who had lost her man. Men groaned who had given their week's pay to some woman who promised to be nice but who slipped away and couldn't be found at the appointed time.

By this time she was just about at the end of her song. She was 'in her sins', as she bellowed out. The bass drum rolled like thunder and the stage lights flickered like forked lightning.

> *'I see the lightning flashing, I hear the waves a dashing*
> *I got to spread the news, I feel this boat a crashing*
> *I got to spread the news, my man is gone and left me*
> *Now I got the stormy sea blues.'*

As the song ends, she feels an understanding with her audience. Their applause is a rich reward. The house is hot. Then she sings again.

Ma Rainey was born in Columbus, Georgia, in 1886. She made her debut in a talent show called *The Bunch of Blackberries* when she was 14, and four years later married travelling show-owner Will Pa Rainey. The couple worked together as Rainey and Rainey, the Assassinators of the Blues, for several years before ultimately separating.

Ma – she always insisted on being called Madame – said she first heard the blues in 1902 in a town in Missouri. She described it as a 'strange and poignant lament' and she concentrated on the blues in her act. No matter what she was singing, her extraordinary contralto voice generated a feeling of melancholy and deep-felt emotion. Of all the Classic blues singers, she was the only one who always sounded down-home, earthy, still part of the communities for whom she sang.

She was noted for her necklace of cold coins, for the gold in her teeth and for the diamonds with which she strewed her considerable person. In big theatres she would have an eagle backdrop and would appear out of a mock phonograph, sparkling with sequins, waving a huge ostrich feather fan or resplendent in a bead head-band. Negro poet Sterling Brown, who saw her live, told British blues historian Paul Oliver:

Ma Rainey was a tremendous figure. She wouldn't have to sing any words; she would moan and the audience would moan with her. She had them in the palm of her hand. I heard Bessie Smith also, but Ma Rainey was the greatest mistress of an audience. Bessie was the greater blues singer, but Ma really knew these people. She weas a person of the folk; she was very simple and direct.

She recorded around 90 songs with a wide variety of accompaniments, from Lovie Austin and Her Blues Serenaders and Fletcher Henderson's Orchestra, through the rural guitar and banjo duet of the Pruitt Twins and the ragtime lilt of Blind Blake, to a jug band led by Georgia Tom. She was one of Paramount's biggest stars and helped build up the label as an unrivalled repository of black jazz and blues recordings. Paramount's *Book of the Blues*, a kind of illustrated who's who of their major artists, enthused romantically:

From the Bottoms of Georgia came the mother of the blues, the Gold Neck Mama of Stageland – Ma Rainey.

From earliest childhood Gertrude Rainey felt that the blues were expressive of the heart of the South and the sad-hearted people who toiled from sunup to sundown, crooning weird tunes to lighten their labors. She took up the stage as a profession, making friends and gaining popularity, not for one moment losing sight of her life ambitions to bring to the North the beautiful melodies of the South and a better understanding of the sorrowful hearts of its people.

After years of appearing in theaters of the South, Ma Rainey went to New York, astounding and bewildering the northerners with what they called 'queer music'. She left and still they did not understand. After a while they began to hear more and more of the delightful music, sung as only Ma Rainey can sing it, and gradually they began to love this type of music as she did.

Ma Rainey taught many blues singers who are so popular today, and is looked up to and worshipped as the true mother of the blues by all her large following.

Her final record was a duet with entertainer Papa Charlie Jackson in 1928. She carried on working for some years, but retired in 1935 to run two theatres she had bought in Georgia. She died in 1939 and is buried in the family plot in Columbus, fondly remembered by those who knew her as remarkably ugly but generous and warm-hearted.

Bessie Smith was also generous and willing to offer help, a quality which led to her being exploited on occasions. There is a story that Ma Rainey helped her get a start in life and, indeed, they worked briefly in the same circus according to researcher Charles Edward Smith who dug out most of the known details about Ma Rainey's life. Ma may have given her a little basic tuition, but no more; according to Georgia Tom, who saw her in 1913, she already had her own, highly individual style.

Bessie Smith, Empress of the
Blues, whose magnificent voice
could make the dreariest pop
song sound like a work of art.

She came from a very poor family in Chattanooga and made her debut as a child singer at the age of nine. She toured with the famous Rabbit Foot Minstrels and by 1919 had her own regular show in a theatre in Atlanta. She arrived in New York in 1923 'tall, fat and scared', according to her producer Frank Walker. There have been rumours for 70 years, fuelled by contemporary newspaper reports, that she made some records in 1921 for both Columbia and Emerson, but nothing has ever turned up. She did, however, audition for Thomas Edison, who wrote her off as no good.

Her first attempts at recording were rejected; no one remembers why, unless she was simply too scared to perform well. But the following day, 16 February 1923, she made 'Down Hearted Blues' and 'Gulf Coast Blues' with Clarence Williams on plodding piano, and the legend was born. The record was a huge success and far superior to most of the dreary cabaret songs masquerading as blues at that time. Walker was impressed enough to offer Bessie a long-term contract.

Williams, a composer, pianist and occasional con man, soon discovered the other side of Bessie Smith when he tricked her into signing with him, instead of Columbia records, and pocketed half her fees. Bessie, a big woman with a fragile temper, went for Clarence, punched him to the floor and trapped him under his desk until he agreed to void the contract.

Columbia did Bessie few favours with her accompaniments in the early years, landing her largely with uninspiring pianists. And they rarely let her rip either; it was 1925 before she was loosed on an up-tempo number, 'Cake Walking Babies from Home', which she and Fletcher Henderson's Hot Six had to record in a tent rigged up inside the studio to assist the new, experimental electrical microphone. It was a great record, but too lively for Frank Walker, and it wasn't released until the 1940s.

Even on the earlier acoustically recorded sides, the enormous, controlled power of her voice comes through. Her duets with Louis Armstrong are durable classics, showing two giant talents at their peak. So are the records she made with trombonist Charlie Green (Trombone Chollie), whose lugubrious tone matched her roughening voice perfectly.

In her heyday Bessie Smith was the highest paid black star of them all. Unlike Ma Rainey, she appealed to black and white audiences and, again unlike Ma, she was physically striking – 'just dripping good looks', according white jazzman Mezz Mezzrow.

Her biographer, Chris Albertson, reports a telling anecdote from singer and dancer Mae Barnes, who was with a company being shown around Windsor Castle by the then Prince of Wales. On seeing a portrait of Queen Mary, Mae remarked, 'What a regal woman'. 'Yes', replied the Prince. 'I believe there are only two truly regal women in this world, my mother and Bessie Smith.'

Bessie spent most of her career on theatre stages and recorded around 160 songs, often second-rate numbers which she transformed by the commitment she brought to the dreariest material. Classic blues historian Derrick Stewart-Baxter summed up her appeal beautifully in a study of the first women singers. 'She was a breathtaking performer and she transformed what we now call the Classic blues into a fresh and intriguing vocal expression. Her achievement was, I believe, unconscious; with her natural genius, she took the vaudeville style of singing, the country blues form and certain jazz elements and these she moulded into a perfect whole. The result was a completely original art form.'

Bessie used her dynamic, rich voice exquisitely, and Billie Holiday, finest of all jazz singers, often said Bessie's ability to carry a word or syllable into the next bar was the basis for her own style.

Bessie even duetted with her arch rival, Clara Smith, and left Clara completely in the shade. She married unwisely, drank more and more gin (and sang about it) and her voice developed a husky edge which many listeners today prefer to the clearer tones of her youth. She kept her reputation as a woman with whom you didn't tangle, but had numerous love affairs with both men and women.

In later years her repertoire was dominated by seedy *double entendre* songs, but even these had that Bessie Smith stamp of authenticity. Her career was effectively killed by the Depression, and although there was one more session in 1933 with a mixed-race swing band, including Benny Goodman, Jack Teagarden, Frankie Newton and Chu Berry, the glory days were over. She died in 1937 from injuries caused by a car crash.

There was as much hype involved in marketing blues as any other form of show business, but no one will argue that Bessie Smith, at least, deserved her title – Empress of the Blues. By the time she died, the Classic blues had long gone. In 1924 the record companies had suddenly discovered that there was another untapped market just wating for them to exploit.

2
Right Where Blues Were Born

Country Blues

Many of the Classic blues singers had started their careers singing anything else but blues. Ida Cox's first song was 'Put Your Arms Around Me Honey', while Alberta Hunter, the 'Idol of Dreamland', included 'Where the River Shannon Flows' in her repertoire. But Ma Rainey had proved there was a demand for the real, down-home blues, as well as the slick, carefully composed songs.

The Classic blues boom led to at least two record labels being set up wholly for black performers – Black Swan in New York, which recorded the first black opera singer, as well as blues competition-winner Trixie Smith, and Sunshine, a tiny Los Angeles operation which issued only three 78s. Two were Classic blues.

There were other, unsuccessful efforts to create black labels, like C and S, which concentrated on black vaudeville, W. C. Handy's own label, and Echo. But

Classic view of Beale Street, Memphis, in 1979, when the street had lain derelict for years. It has now been refurbished as a major tourist attraction.

Okeh Records, which had started it all, slowly realized the need to market its black artists to the black communities, and in 1921 issued the first black blues and jazz listing. At first it was simply called the 'Colored Catalog', but in 1922 Okeh introduced a term which was adopted and used by the record industry for more than 20 years: race records.

One of the most important race record labels – perhaps *the* most important – began as an offshoot of a furniture company. The Wisconsin Chair Company of Port Washington also made phonographs and cabinets, and it seemed a natural progression to start making the records as well. They called their label Paramount, and the first blues released were two Lucille Hegamin sides leased from another label.

In 1922 they set up a special 12000 series, which was reserved for black talent, yet with all this activity, there were only 50 blues records issued in 1921 and another 50 in 1922. Buyers wanted more. Unfortunately, there were too few singers around and their records were being issued on numerous labels. While Bessie Smith and Ma Rainey were contracted to one company, lesser talents sang for anyone who wanted them. Edna Hicks appeared on seven labels in one year, and Rosa Henderson, Lena Wilson and Hazel Meyers on six each. A 1924 Paramount catalogue even appealed to customers to come up with suggestions of singers to record.

That same year they signed up Ma Rainey and took over the ailing Black Swan label. Paramount's white

owners may have been totally cynical about their black records, but they built up a mail-order business and employed Mayo Williams, a black, as manager of the race artists series. But it was obvious that talent would have to be sought outside the main centres of New York and Chicago.

Okeh talent scout Ralph Peer made the first field recording trip in 1923 when he went to Atlanta, Georgia, to record white country musician Fiddlin' John Carson. While he was there, he also auditioned blues singers Lucille Bogan, a very fine, tough-voiced singer with a long career ahead of her, and the less interesting Fannie Goosby. A coupling of one song by each of them made up the first race record to be recorded on location.

Until 1926, most field recordings were devoted to Classic singers (Ada Brown and Mary Bradford in St Louis; Lela Bolden and Ruth Green in New Orleans; Sara Martin and Viola Baker in Atlanta) and vaudeville (Butterbeans and Susie, Billy and Mary Mack, Sloppy Henry). But on the April 1924 trip to Atlanta, Peer recorded two sides which marked another landmark in the blues. They were the first country blues, a fairly undistinguished coupling by one Ed Andrews, which Okeh claimed were recorded 'right where blues songs were born'. A nice line, but the record didn't sell. There had been two guitar solos recorded a few months earlier by sophisticated Louisville performer Sylvester Weaver, who had previously accompanied Sara Martin, but Andrews' 'Barrelhouse Blues' was the first recorded vocal.

Atlanta went on to become a major blues recording centre, not just for locally based artists, but also for musicians from Texas, Alabama, Mississippi, Tennessee and South Carolina.

The first self-accompanied male blues singer to become a record star was the unlikely figure of Papa Charlie Jackson, a banjo-guitar (banjo body, guitar tuning) player and minstrel show entertainer, who made his first record for Paramount in 1924. Paramount was still in the experimental stage, issuing records in the hope of finding a market, and with Papa Charlie they struck lucky. Paramount's *Book of the Blues* stated confidently:

From the ancient historical city of New Orleans came Charlie Jackson, a witty, cheerful, kind-hearted man, who, with his joyous-sounding voice and his banjo, sang and strummed his way into the hearts of thousands of people.

PAPA CHARLIE JACKSON
Complete Recorded Works In Chronological Order

document RECORDS
DOCD-5087

VOL. 1 * 1924 to February 1926

Papa Charlie Jackson, an
amiable entertainer who
made the first recordings of
a number of blues standards.

When he first contracted to sing and play for Paramount, many pessimistic persons laughed and said they were certain no one wanted to hear comedy songs sung by a man strumming a banjo. But it wasn't long before they realized how wrong they were. Charlie and his records took the entire country by storm, and now people like nothing better than to come home after a tiring and busy day and play his records.

His hearty voice and gay, harmonious strumming on the banjo causes their cares and worries to dwindle away and gives them a careful frame of mind and makes life one sweet song.

Like all Paramount records, Papa Charlie's were made from inferior material, which generated surface noise even when new. As one employee admitted in later years, 'They even had static in 'em when they were new'. But they sold, often by mail order or by a somewhat ramshackle distribution system, one salesman travelling 2,000 miles a week.

Like other entertainers loosely classified as blues singers, Papa Charlie's repertoire ranged through comedy songs like 'The Cat's Got the Measles', ballads, hokum, straight blues, jazz with the Freddie Keppard

and Tiny Parham bands, and duets with Paramount stars Ida Cox, Ma Rainey and Blind Blake. He was the first on record with blues standards such as 'Shake That Thing', 'Alabama Bound', and 'All I Want Is a Spoonful', and while his records are scarcely deep or emotional, they are still highly enjoyable.

Paramount pushed them hard. In 1927 there was an advert asking fans, 'Have you heard about the twitching, shaking, shimmying, throbbing, sobbing sensational new dance, Skoodle um Skoo? Papa Charlie Jackson, the one and only Papa Charlie, tells about it in his latest Paramount release.' Why Paramount dropped Jackson in 1930 after he had recorded nearly 70 songs for them isn't clear, but by the time of a final issued session for Okeh in 1934, his sound was very outdated. He died around 1938, an unlikely trailblazer.

Paramount's mail-order customers asked for more country blues, and in 1925 Mayo Williams was recommended by Paramount dealer R. T. Ashford in Dallas, Texas, to hear a fat, itinerant blind singer and guitar player called Lemon Jefferson. He was summoned to Chicago (Paramount couldn't afford field trips) and recorded two dull spirituals as Deacon L. J. Bates. A few months later Lemon was back in the studio recording four blues, the like of which had never been heard on record. Sales were phenomenal and Jefferson recorded every few months for the next four years, selling an estimated million records.

It's no wonder that singers from Leadbelly and Josh White to Lightnin' Hopkins and T-Bone Walker were all eager to claim they had led Blind Lemon around (like other blind singers, he seemed remarkably self-sufficient), or that his songs, or lines from them, appeared in many later records.

British writer Bob Groom has traced part of Lemon's 'Dry Southern Blues' to Robert Johnson's 'Love in Vain' and 'Walking Blues'; his 'Black Horse Blues' to Tommy Johnson's 'Black Mare Blues' and Charley Patton's 'Pony Blues', and his 'Black Snake Blues' (possibly in turn lifted from Victoria Spivey) to Big Joe Williams' 'Crawling King Snake'. There are many more examples in records by Isaiah Nettles (the 'Mississippi Moaner'), Shorty Bob Parker, Sleepy John Estes and Lightnin' Hopkins, among numerous others.

Lemon was a guitar player of considerable skill and dexterity in a style that defied copyists, and a singer with a high, clear, whining voice. His songs were full of vivid imagery of sex, imprisonment and execution, drink

Blind Lemon Jefferson, whose
success led to many other
country bluesmen being recorded.

and occasional humour. Stephen Calt and Gayle Dean Wardlow, two of the most indefatigable blues researchers, wrote in a history of Paramount Records:

In accompanying himself, Jefferson tried to concoct a new guitar riff to accompany each vocal phrase, playing as fast as his fingers could move. The ordinary blues guitarists of the period used a single guitar fill, repeated ad infinitum after each vocal phrase. Jefferson brought fresh melodic and dynamic variations of his vocal delivery, which was probably the most flexible of any recorded blues singer in history.

Paramount's ever-trusty *Book of the Blues* pulled out all the stops for Lemon.

Can anyone imagine a fate more horrible than to find that one is blind? Such was the heart-rending fate of Lemon Jefferson, who was born blind and realized as a small child that life had withheld one glorious joy from him – sight. The environment began to play its important part in his destiny. He could hear and he heard the sad-hearted, weary people of his homeland, Dallas, singing weird, sad melodies at their work and play, and unconsciously, he began to imitate them, lamenting his fate in song. He learned to play a guitar and for years he entertained his friends freely, moaning his weird songs as a means for forgetting his affliction.

Lemon stayed with Paramount for the whole of his recording career, apart from an odd venture to Okeh, which was rapidly halted with legal threats. He recorded at least 100 songs and died mysteriously in 1929 in Chicago. His body was taken back to Texas by blues pianist Will Ezell, and was buried at Wortham, not far from Couchman where he was born.

It was Lemon's success more than Papa Charlie's which sparked off the chase to record country blues. Lemon was virtually uncopyable, so every company started looking for obscure blues singers who might unlock the same sales figures.

Paramount themselves struck lucky yet again, this time signing up Blind Blake from Florida, a warm-voiced, ordinary singer, but a ragtime guitarist with few equals. His real name was probably Arthur Blake (one record was issued as Blind Arthur) and in six years he recorded 84 titles under his own name and dozens more as accompanist to many Paramount artists. His guitar

Blind Arthur Blake, a
wistful singer but a ragtime
guitarist with few equals.

artistry was breathtaking, equalled on record by perhaps Willie Walker from South Carolina (described by many East Coast bluesmen as the best ever) and Blind Gary Davis, but very few others.

He played in a rhythmic dance style, full of delightful inventions, and was as much at home with a small New Orleans group led by Johnny Dodds as he was duetting with banjo player Gus Cannon. He travelled widely, drank heavily, sold lots of superlative records and his influence can be heard even today in the playing of numerous guitarists, black and white. When and where he died is unknown for certain.

The Paramount *Book of the Blues* waxed even more poetically about Blake than it did for Lemon Jefferson.

We have all heard expressions of people 'singing in the rain' or 'laughing in the face of adversity', but we never saw such a good example of it until we came upon the history of Blind Blake.

Born in Jacksonville in sunny Florida, he seems to have absorbed some of the sunny atmosphere, disregarding the fact that nature had cruelly denied him a vision of outer things. He could not see the things that others saw, but he had a better gift. A gift of an inner vision that allowed him to see things more beautiful. The pictures that he alone could see made him long to express them in some way, so he turned to music.

He studied long and earnestly, listening to talented pianists and guitar players, and began to gradually draw out harmonious tunes to fit every mood. Now that he is recording exclusively for Paramount, the public has the benefit of his talent and agrees with one body that he has an unexplainable gift of making one laugh or cry as he feels, and sweet chords and tunes that come down from his talking guitar express a feeling of his moods.

Paramount never found any artists to match Ma Rainey, Charlie Jackson, Lemon Jefferson or Blind Blake in terms of sales, but they certainly found some extraordinary talent. These people might not have sold many records originally, but their output has been sought eagerly by collectors ever since.

In 1926 Paramount tried James Jackson, a street musician, discovered in Birmingham, Alabama, who had a high, raucous voice and aggressive slide guitar style. Paramount scout Harry Charles sold him to Paramount as Bo Weavil Jackson and immediately afterwards to Vocalion as Sam Butler. Whatever the name, his quirky mix of blues, spirituals and reworked ballads didn't sell.

Another Birmingham singer, Buddy Boy Hawkins, was given a chance in 1927 and, according to Harry Charles, was so petrified by the recording process, he spoiled numerous takes by pulling back from the microphone. Hawkins recorded 12 titles over two sessions (the last shared with Charley Patton, who can be heard encouraging him on one track), but Charles thought little of him and he was never heard of again. Yet he was a strong, husky-voiced singer and a very accomplished guitarist, whose 'Jailhouse Fire Blues' is among the very best recorded in the 1920s. He also gave Paramount one of the strangest numbers it recorded – 'Voice Throwing Blues' – an attempt at ventriloquism on a version of 'Hesitating Blues' in which Hawkins sings two parts. Even in Paramount mono the effect is startling.

But it wasn't just Paramount hunting for the new Lemon Jefferson, of course. From 1926 onwards, the big companies like Victor, Okeh, Columbia, Brunswick, Gennett and Vocalion sent recording teams to the main centres of the South, recording virtually everyone who seemed to have a couple of songs and a modicum of talent. The results obviously give an unbalanced impression of blues at this time. The records issued owed a lot to the tastes of the producers, as well as the buying audi-

ence, and every interview with elderly blues singers who did record is studded with the names of unknowns who were claimed to be as good as, if not better than, those who made it. It's undoubtedly true, as field recordings in the rich blues areas in the 1960s showed, throwing up talented older men like Fred McDowell and Cat Iron who had never recorded before.

A lot depended on pure chance: a singer just happened to be in town when a recording unit was there, or he just happened to play where a talent scout heard him. There were also accidents and technical problems; two whole sessions of 12 numbers by J. T. 'Funny Papa' Smith at Forth Worth, Texas, were wrecked by faulty masters, for instance.

The main recording centres were Memphis, New Orleans, Dallas and Atlanta, crossroad cities where blacks leaving the rural life naturally headed. Other venues included St Louis, Missouri; San Antonio, Texas; Birmingham, Alabama; Columbia, South Carolina; and Charlotte, North Carolina. Between 1927 and 1930 there were 11 recording sessions in Memphis, seven in New Orleans, eight in Dallas, and 17 in Atlanta alone.

Memphis in particular was one of the richest seedbeds for black musical talents in the 1920s. It was the main centre for a wide area, a shipping point for cotton, an important railhead, and a fairly easy road journey from the Delta area of Mississippi. Some migrants used Memphis as a stopping place on their way north to St Louis and Chicago; others stayed to give the place a reputation for violence, lawlessness and a remarkable spread of music. You could find it on Beale Street in its notorious bars, gambling halls and pool rooms, or in Handy Park on a sunny day. Bengt Olsson, who did much research in the town in 1969, says, 'Beale Street was a rough, tough gambling, whoring, cutting, musical living street'. No one was safe there after dark, and the grim joke in Pee Wee's, the most famous musicians' bar, was that they couldn't close until someone had been killed. Other bars or pool rooms remembered by Memphis bluesmen were the Monarch, the Hole in the Wall, and the Panama.

The heyday of Beale Street was the 1920s and early 1930s. By the Second World war, its fearsome reputation had turned it into a tourist attraction.

Memphis mayor E. H. Crump tried to stamp out the vice in Beale Street in 1908 but with little success, apart from being satirized in Frank Stokes's 1927 blues 'Mr

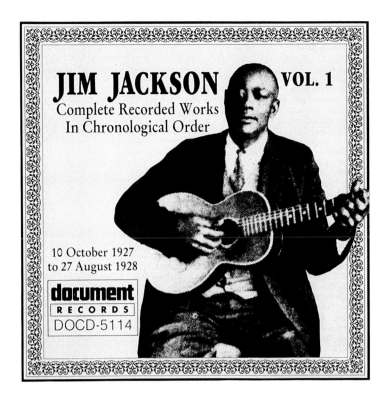

Songster Jim Jackson whose 'Kansas
City Blues' was an enormous hit.
His recordings are a valuable
treasure trove of the songs of a
previous generation.

records include few straight blues, concentrating instead on old minstrel songs and formal, composed songs from the turn of the century. Paul Oliver described his output as 'one of the richest stores of traditional songs,' and his deep voice and basic guitar have an enduring quality about them.

By the time Victor recorded him, Jackson had already waxed his version of 'Kansas City Blues', which may have sold up to a million copies, plus two sequels. Another follow-up 'I'm Gonna Move to Louisiana', was the same song with a different destination.

A few of his songs were actually medleys of older tunes, which add to their historical value, and he was a dab hand at disguising satirical digs at whites and the police in pieces like 'What a Time', 'Bye Bye Policemen' and 'Traveling Man'. Jackson's last record in 1930 coupled 'Hesitation Blues' and 'St Louis Blues', two of the folk themes which W. C. Handy had adapted from an earlier tradition. He died in Mississippi in 1937.

The most impressive of the Memphis singers was Frank Stokes, who had a powerful, rich voice and a guitar style which showed a strong ragtime influence. He played in a duo called the Beale Street Sheiks with

Crump Don't Like It'. Another Memphis character who appeared in a blues was Jim Kinnane, who ran some of the roughest joints in town and was celebrated by Robert Wilkins in 'Old Jim Canan's'.

Musicians from miles around congregated in Memphis, and the field recording outfits, especially Victor, found rich pickings. On its first trip in February 1927, Victor recorded the Memphis Jug Band; the ethereal gospel singer Blind Mamie Forehand and her guitarist husband; Ollie Rupert, a female singer whose two songs were accompanied by Jew's harp, and several other minor artists. A second session the following year attracted some of the most respected names in blues: songster Jim Jackson, Cannon's Jug Stompers, gospel ravers Lonnie McIntorsh and Elder Richard Bryant, the Memphis Jug Band, Frank Stokes, Rosie Mae Moore, Tommy Johnson, Ishmon Bracey and Arthur Petties. A third trip added Furry Lewis, Bessie Tucker, Ida May Mack, Will Shade, Robert Wilkins and Charlie Kyle to the roster.

Jim Jackson was a very popular figure from Hernando, Mississippi, who spent most of his time travelling with the medicine shows. Pianist Speckled Red recalled him as 'a big fat feller' who sang, danced and told jokes. His

Frank Stokes, a rich-voiced Memphis
blacksmith whose wonderful records
of blues and earlier songs are deeply
prized by discerning collectors.

Memphis singer Furry Lewis (left), who recorded blues and ballads in the twenties. He lived long enough to appear in a Hollywood movie, and be serenaded by Joni Mitchell.

Oh play that thing! The superb Memphis Jug Band (right) in full swing in the twenties.

flat-pick guitarist Dan Sane, who was also a member of the South Memphis Jug Band, led by another superb singer, Jack Kelly.

Stokes and Sane had recorded for Paramount before Victor found them, and their repertoire included older pre-blues songs like 'You Shall', 'Chicken You Can Roost Behind the Moon' and 'I Got Mine'. One of the best was a two-part version of "Tain't Nobody's Business If I Do", another pre-blues song probably better known in the jazzier version by Bessie Smith.

The Beale Street Sheiks perfected the rolling, two-guitar style for which Memphis was noted, the two instruments meshing like gears with total precision. It was also found in the work of Garfield Akers and Joe Callicott, and Memphis Minnie and Kansas Joe McCoy, but the Sheiks were really a partnership without equal. Stokes also used South Memphis Jug Band violinist Will Batts on his last two sessions, producing at least one wistful masterpiece in the moving 'Shiney Town Blues'. Thankfully, 40 of his brilliant recordings survive to dazzle new generations.

Another fine performer was Robert Wilkins, again a Mississippi singer who had moved to Memphis. He recorded for Victor and Vocalion, and his first record, a two-part 'Rolling Stone' was an astonishing, hypnotic piece that maintained momentum remorselessly against a weird guitar figure. Wilkins revealed in later years that the strange sound was accidental, caused by a guitar damaged on the way to the studio.

His other records include a number with haunting tunes like 'Police Sergeant Blues' and 'That's No Way to Get Along'. His 1964 reworking of the latter into a religious song (he was the Reverend Robert Wilkins by then) was covered by the Rolling Stones.

The other widely recorded Memphis singer was one-legged Walter 'Furry' Lewis, who survived to be fêted by white collectors in the 1960s, and even serenaded ('Furry Sings the Blues') by Joni Mitchell. He had a pleasing, unforced voice with strong vibrato, often using slide to create effect, as well as a rolling rhythm which owed much to the Delta style. His recorded repertoire included some tough blues, but also rare, full-length ver-

sion of ballads like 'Billy Lyons and Stack O'Lee', 'Kassie Jones' and 'John Henry'.

Allen Shaw, Tom Dickson, Minnie Wallace, Reuben Lacey, Lewis Black, Mooch Richardson, T. C. Johnson and 'Blue Coat' Tom Nelson were just a few of the many and varied singers who recorded in Memphis. Some made just two sides and vanished. Others recorded briefly and carried on with their lives, sometimes surviving to be lionized in their old age by white collectors. But Memphis was also known for the jug bands.

Jug bands probably arose from the way that poorer musicians made their own instruments from cigar boxes, tins, broom handles and anything else that came to hand. A child's toy, the kazoo, was popular and was recorded in some unlikely settings (Tampa Red, a brilliant guitarist who recorded in Chicago and New York, ruined some of his best records with it). Washboards, with their ridged edges played with thimbles, were very popular for rhythm, and by blowing across the neck of a bottle or jug, a skilled player with a lot of breath control could create a fruity, resonant sound like a small tuba.

Jug bands may have evolved formally in Louisville, Kentucky, where Whistler and His Jug Band, the talented Clifford Hayes, and Phillips Louisville Jug Band stood on the divide between blues and jazz.

In Memphis, jug bands that played all kinds of music for all occasions were very popular, and the best were the Memphis Jug Band, Cannon's Jug Stompers and the South Memphis Jug Band.

The Memphis Jug Band (MJB) was founded by Will Shade (also known as Son Brimmer), and Furry Lewis claimed to have played in the first version around 1925. The MJB had a varying line-up and recorded heavily between 1927 and 1934 in a wide variety of styles. There were straight blues, old minstrel songs, waltzes, a touch of jazz and even a really beautiful close-harmony number called 'K. C. Moan'. Memphis Minnie sang with them, as did the excellent Hattie Hart and the acid-voiced Minnie Wallace, among others, and there were offshoots like the Picaninny Jug Band and solos by various group members.

It was very enjoyable, good-time music on the whole,

Gus Cannon (left), Banjo Joe on his first records, who led the finest Memphis jug band and recorded some archaic songs among the blues and dance tunes.

Tommy Johnson (above), a sad alcoholic, who recorded a handful of deeply sensitive and highly influential songs like 'Big Road Blues' and 'Canned Heat Blues'.

but Gus Cannon's Jug Stompers offered a bit more. Cannon first recorded as Banjo Joe, but the jug band sides, with the brilliant harmonica player Noah Lewis, were in a class of their own. Cannon was one of the oldest singers to record, and his 'Feather Bed Blues' contains verses referring to the American Civil War. The band left a superb legacy of ragtime novelty songs, but most of all blues, and one number, 'Walk Right In', became a major hit for the Rooftop Singers in the 1960s.

The South Memphis Jug Band was really a blues band with occasional jug, led by street musician Jack Kelly, who had one of the best blues voices on record. Kelly turned out a superb set of 24 band and solo sides, enhanced by Dan Sane and Will Batts' evocative violin, and even surfaced briefly on the post-war Sun label before disappearing forever.

Harmonica player Jed Davenport also had a jug band which accompanied Memphis Minnie, but it never enjoyed the success of the other three.

While the big recording companies were trawling

Memphis and elsewhere, Paramount had been busy in its studios in Chicago and Grafton, Wisconsin. They had recorded Frank Stokes and Gus Cannon, but their greatest finds had been unearthed by Henry C. Speir, a record shop owner in Jackson, Mississippi, who acted as talent scout for all the major labels.

Paramount had recorded some very uncommercial artists sent up by Speir, including singing tamale salesman Moses Mason and blind street singer Joe Reynolds. Few made more than a side or two – many had only a few songs in their repertoire. They might be highly regarded by modern collectors, but they were commercial flops.

Speir had sent Victor the Jackson area bluesmen Tommy Johnson and Ishmon Bracey, a raucous female singer called Rosie Mae Moore, and singer-guitarist Charlie McCoy, an associate of the singing Chatmon family, who recorded under numerous names like the Mississippi Sheiks, the Mississippi Black Snakes and the Mississippi Mud Steppers.

Johnson was an alcholic wanderer with a gentle,

Charley Patton, epitome of the hard-edged, rhythmic Delta blues. His singing was intense to the point of incoherence, his guitar playing powerful and urgent. The most admired of all the early singers by white collectors.

tremulous voice that used high falsetto to great effect over a walking bass rhythm – the whole perfectly integrated. His songs, like 'Cool Drink of Water Blues', 'Big Road Blues' and 'Maggie Campbell', were enormously influential and in many ways unique – certainly far removed from the rough vigour of the Delta style. Bracey was similar in style, although with a more nasal voice. Neither sold well on Victor, and by the time they reached Paramount, both had exhausted their best material, and Johnson was virtually disabled by alcohol.

Then, in 1929, Speir sent Paramount probably his greatest discovery – a small, light-skinned man with a ferocious delivery – Charley Patton.

Patton's music was already a bit old-fashioned when he first recorded, but it was what the buyers wanted to

hear. He was frequently incoherent, the force of his music running words into a verbal traffic jam – a habit not helped by his thick accent and hoarse voice. Even his companion, Son House, wasn't sure what he was singing about on occasions.

He was an intense, argumentative figure who readily got involved in fights, but who had songs for every kind of audience. He sang gospel, jumbled versions of white pop songs, ballads about the boll weevil, and blues about the people around him. It's possible his father was Henderson Chatmon, head of the musical Chatmon family, although Sam Chatmon, his half-brother, preferred the more sophisticated music of the Chatmons to Charley's, which he described scathingly as sounding like somebody choking to death.

Patton often played with a slide, using it to punctuate his half-finished verses or underscore the percussive, driving rhythms he generated. Much of his music was impossible to imitate, many of his songs had little textual relevance outside a small area of Mississippi, yet he was popular enough for Paramount to record 41 songs in just one year.

One recording that did have wider interest was a very big seller, the vivid, two-part 'High Water Everywhere', which recounted the devastation caused by the 1927 Mississippi floods. It was a disaster also commemorated on record by Barbecue Bob in Atlanta and Bessie Smith, although with none of the descriptive power that Patton offered.

Patton's biographers, Stephen Calt and Gayle Dean Wardlow, dismiss suggestions that Patton influenced any other singers, not even associates Son House, Willie Brown and Kid Bailey. His songs were recorded by others: his style wasn't.

But it was Patton who got Son House his first recording session at which he made three two-part blues and an unissued version of 'Walking Blues', which amazingly survived as a test pressing, discovered by luck in 1986.

House sang with the declamatory fervour of a preacher with slashing bottleneck accompaniment, but wasn't asked back. He didn't record again until a Library of Congress team caught up with him at Lake Cormorant, Mississippi, 11 years later, when he performed a long and varied selection – some with Willie Brown, Patton's old partner, who had also recorded for Paramount with little success. So had Louise Johnson, a fine barrelhouse pianist, whose records have House and Brown cheering her on in the backround.

Patton's last records were made in 1934 with his singer wife, Bertha Lee. Few were issued, and those that were show a cooling of the old flame, a tiredness, especially on the reworking of earlier sides, which indicated the heart ailment soon to kill him. Whatever his role in the history of the blues, Patton remains the epitomy of the dark, Delta sound with its anguished vocals and heavy accompaniments.

Hundreds of miles away in Atlanta, Georgia, music was being recorded which was far removed from the harsh Delta blues. This was a big area for hillbilly music, and the blues of the area reflect some influence from white music. They are lighter, less emotionally involved on the whole, and with more emphasis on technique rather than effect.

Blind Willie McTell from Georgia, who recorded music of great delicacy and skill on his huge Stella 12-string guitar.

Like Memphis, Atlanta was a sporting town with razor gangs and wild bars around Decatur Street, and plenty of opportunities for musicians from Georgia, the Carolinas, Alabama and Virginia. The finest of the lot and one of the most important figures in all American folk music was Blind Willie McTell.

McTell was born near Thompson, Georgia, and was blind from birth. He favoured the unwieldy 12-string guitar and was even more proficient on it than Leadbelly, the Texas songster. He first recorded in 1927, and for the last time in 1956. He sang blues, gospel, minstrel show songs, white hillbilly, ballads, vaudeville – anything for which anyone would pay him. He also changed names as easily as he changed record companies, recording as Georgia Bill, Blind Sammy and Pig and Whistle Red, among others.

His early work includes some of the most poignant and beautiful blues ever recorded, particularly the haunting 'Mama 'Tain't Long Fo' Day', with lyrics of real poetry echoed by delicate slide accompaniment. It is mesmerizing music of the highest order. Some of his other classics include 'Travelin' Blues', a guitar show-case which allows McTell to imitate train sounds, voices and piano, and a set of gospel songs with wife Kate in 1935. His Library of Congress recordings emphasized his repertoire of older songs, like 'Delia', 'Dyin' Crapshooter's Blues' and 'Murderer's Home', but McTell was a brilliant and skilled craftsman in all he did.

Twelve-string guitars were also favoured by Bob and Charlie Hicks, brothers who recorded as Barbecue Bob and Charley Lincoln. Bob, a delightful singer and fast, percussive slide guitarist, was Columbia's big star for several years until the Depression and, like McTell, recorded a wide range of material. Charley Lincoln was less gifted, his voice sourer and less flexible. His trade-

mark was a maniacal laugh, a bit forced on his own records, but heard to best effect on a superb coupling with the brother's friend, Nellie Florence. Another singer, the mysterious Willie Baker, performed in Bob's style, but is a complete biographical blank, like so many rural singers.

McTell's regular partner, until the 1950s, was Curley Weaver, whose mother, Dip, taught the Hicks boys their individual style. Strangely, Curley rarely adopted it, apart from his showcase 'No No Blues'.

Weaver was involved with the young harmonica player Eddie Mapp – cruelly murdered before he could fully develop his talents – and Fred McMullen, another mystery man, who was equally adept at slide guitar and fancy fingerpicking.

A fourth member of the group was Buddy Moss, a younger guitarist and harmonica player, who recorded with Barbecue Bob and Weaver as the very exciting Georgian Cotton Pickers, and with McMullen and Weaver as the Georgia Browns. Moss went on to have a long recording career, but was more closely associated

Barbecue Bob, one of the two singing Hicks Brothers and a highly effective 12-string slide guitarist. He made a big selling series of delightful records but died young.

Buddy Moss, who played with Barbecue Bob and Curley Weaver and made dozens of quality records in the late thirties. He was recorded in the blues revival but seemed to have little success.

BARBECUE BOB
(ROBERT HICKS)

Complete Recorded Works
In Chronological Order
VOLUME 1
25 March 1927 to 13 April 1928

document
RECORDS
DOCD-5046

with the sound of North Carolina's Blind Boy Fuller than the Atlanta guitarists.

A very different sound was produced by Joshua 'Peg Leg' Howell, a one-legged busker whose songs represent an older era, and with considerable white influence at times. Columbia said of him: 'When Peg Leg Howell lost a leg, the world gained a great singer of blues. The loss of a leg never bothered Peg Leg as far as chasing round after blues is concerned. He sure catches them and stomps all over them.'

He certainly did when playing with his Gang, guitarist Henry Williams and off-key alley fiddler Eddie Anthony, on numbers like 'Turkey Buzzard Blues', a reworking of 'Turkey in the Straw'. But his sensitive solo, 'Skin Game Blues', with its unusual structure and plaintive tune, is a much-prized item.

There were many names recorded at this time, and many types of blues. You could buy archaic pan-pipe-accompanied country dances by Henry Thomas, a travelling player known as Ragtime Texas. There was the extraordinary George 'Bullet' Williams, who screamed through his nose as he blew wild harmonica, and animal imitations from Freeman Stowers. There were the curious Nugrape Twins in Atlanta, hymning the delights of religion and a non-alcholic drink, and outdated remnants of the past like Alec Johnson's coon songs and the homespun humour of Beans Hambone. There were also highly skilled ragtime guitarists like barber William Moore from Virginia and South Carolina's Willie Walker.

Many, many artists recorded once and were never heard of again. Some were luckier. Sam Collins from the Louisiana–Mississippi borderlands, recorded more than 20 sides, with many more unissued, between 1927 and 1931. He played out-of-tune slide guitar, which actually sounded quite good, paired with an eerie high voice that gained him the nickname 'Cryin' Sam Collins. There was some similarity with Bo Weavil Jackson from Alabama, and certainly with King Solomon Hill, another singer who used high falsetto to stunning effect and who sang with Collins and Lemon Jefferson on occasions. (King Solomon Hill was actually Joe Holmes, whom Gayle Dean Wardlow discovered had taken his name from a local church.)

There may have been some contact between Collins, Holmes and Willard 'Rambling' Thomas, a Louisiana singer recorded by Paramount in the search for a new Lemon Jefferson. Thomas sang with Blind Lemon, and it

is thought Holmes did too, as he recorded one of several tributes issued on Lemon's death, while there are musical links between the styles of Collins and Thomas.

Mississippi John Hurt doesn't really seem linked with anyone. He recorded 13 ballads, light blues and gospel songs in a gentle, warm voice for Okeh – and that was it. He carried on as a farmer and playing for dances in Avalon, Mississippi, until someone thought of looking for him there in 1963 because he had sung an 'Avalon Blues'. He became a much-loved figure in the blues revival and recorded extensively (and with fewer signs of old age than any other rediscovered early singer) until his death in 1966.

The Delta may have been the home of William Harris, a big-voiced shouter with a complex, rhythmic guitar style, who was reportedly a minstrel show entertainer. He was an impressive singer, but little more is known about him. Roosevelt Graves and his brother Uaroy came from central Mississippi and recorded 21 country band and gospel sides. They were another Speir discovery, and their 1936 sides as the Mississippi Jook

Mississippi John Hurt (left), a gentle voiced singer, was rediscovered in Avalon, the town he serenaded in his only pre-war sessions in 1928.

Skip James (right), a highly gifted singer, guitarist and pianist who made one marathon session for Paramount in the twenties but had a good second career after he was rediscovered in the sixties. He even toured Europe but remained an enigmatic and bitter man.

Band are superb and rare examples of an exuberant kind of music seldom captured on record. A bigger mystery were the Two Poor Boys – Joe Evans and Arthur McClain – who are thought to have been from Tennessee and whose output could be that of a white hillbilly band.

Another widely recorded artist was Ed Bell from Alabama, who was picked up by Paramount in 1927, with further sides for QRS with relaxed Louisville bluesman Clifford Gibson in 1929. It now seems fairly certain that Bell also recorded as Barefoot Bill and Sluefoot Joe, which makes a total of 24 first-class country blues. Bell was a typical travelling player, who eventually turned to the church and died in 1966.

One of the most talented and enigmatic of all the performers Speir sent to Paramount was the eccentric singer, guitarist and pianist Nehemiah 'Skip' James. He shared the high, expressive falsetto style of Sam Collins and King Solomon Hill, but he came from Bentonia in Mississippi, where he had learned a startling, quickfire guitar style from the unrecorded Henry Stuckey, who in turn said *he'd* picked it up from Bahamian soldiers in First World War France.

Skip James had just one pre-war session, and turned out an astonishing 18 sides, five with guitar and five with piano. 'I'm So Glad' in particular was a remarkable masterpiece – simple words but accompanied by incredibly fast and accurate finger-picked guitar. His piano playing was even more sensational and a bit bizarre; indeed, there is nothing else like it on record, as he pounds the keyboard and a board placed beneath his feet to emphasize his foot stomping. One number, '22–20 Blues', was made up on the spot after the producer asked if he knew anything like Roosevelt Sykes's '44 Blues'. James promptly invented a song about a non-existent calibre of gun, and it included a spectacular piano break with wild keyboard runs.

Paramount were impressed, but Skip James was never called back. He was tracked down in the 1960s after a very long search and had a good second career, although he remained brooding and bitter.

But who knows what talent escaped the record companies, and who all the artists that are merely named in the discographies really were? Take Geeshie Wiley, a singer and guitarist, for instance. She recorded just six titles with Elvie Thomas in 1930 and 1931, and is one of the few female country blues artists on record. She *might* have come from near Natchez, Mississippi, she *might* have lived in Jackson, and *might* have played guitar and ukulele in a medicine show. Other than that, one of the best country blues singers on record is just a handful of scratchy, barely audible, rare 78s and a big reputation among a small number of collectors.

3
How Long, How Long Blues

Depression and Recovery

The most important recording centre for country blues outside Memphis and Atlanta was Dallas, Texas. Columbia went there first in 1927, picking up Coley Jones and his Dallas String Band, harmonica player William McCoy, the unique dolceola (a variety of dulcimer with piano keys) player Washington Phillips, and Blind Willie Johnson, a magnificent gospel shouter and superb guitarist. There were other more minor figures, too, like Lillian Glinn, Billiken Johnson, Gertrude Perkins and Hattie Hudson. Most of them returned the following year, with the addition of Willie Reed, a fine, rural singer-guitarist, most of whose output remains unissued, Otis Harris, Jewell Nelson and another string band, Frenchy's.

Victor's most important finds were Sammy Hill, Jesse 'Babyface' Thomas (brother of Rambling Thomas and much recorded in post-war years) and Bessie Tucker, a

Meade Lux Lewis recorded the milestone boogie, 'Honky Tonk Train Blues', in 1927, but didn't record again for eight years. One of the famed Boogie Woogie Trio with Pete Johnson and Albert Ammons.

dark-voiced, sombre woman who sang evocatively about violence, prostitution and jail with apparent first-hand knowledge. When Paul Oliver went looking for her and Ida May Mack in 1960 he was told, 'They're tough cookies, don't mess with them'.

Brunswick and Vocalion did quite well in Dallas, too, recording Texas Tommy, Blind Norris, Gene Campbell and Jake Jones, among others, but there were no performers here on the level of the best of the Memphis and Atlanta discoveries.

The most important of the Texas singers had, in fact, been taken to New York for his debut in 1927, and his sessions alternated between the North and Texas for the next six years. Alger 'Texas' Alexander didn't play an instrument, but was accompanied by a variety of musicians, many struggling to keep up with his long, irregular lines which were derived directly from work songs and field hollers. Lonnie Johnson, a sophisticated and

immensely talented guitarist, had the flexibility to respond best to Alexander's primitive sound, developing a free style which sometimes seemed to cope simply by ignoring Alexander's rough vocals.

Okeh also used Little Hat Jones, a central Texas bluesman with a strange trademark of opening songs at double tempo before slowing down to the right speed, the white guitarist Eddie Lang who sounded rather baffled, despite his sympathy for black music, New Orleans jazzman King Oliver, and even the Mississippi Sheiks, who managed to get Alexander as near to swinging as he ever got.

Alexander recorded heavily and left a legacy of rich, if generally sombre, imagery. He made one record after the Second World War, but is also thought to have made a test disc accompanied by his younger cousin, Lightnin' Hopkins. The grim old man frightened the woman who was auditioning them and nothing came of it.

The parochialism of some of the rural singers made them difficult to sell in the North, where migrant blacks were trying to set up a new life in the cities. They still wanted the blues, but on themes to which they could respond, and in a slicker style which reflected their new urbanization.

Lonnie Johnson, who first recorded in 1925 as violinist with Charlie Creath's Jazz-o-Maniacs, was the ultimate

No one moaned like Alger 'Texas' Alexander whose primitive field holler vocals were backed by the cream of jazz and blues accompanists.

Lonnie Johnson, possibly the most gifted of all bluesmen and equally at home with Duke Ellington or Texas Alexander.

city entertainer. He was slick, intelligent, well dressed and the master of a remarkable number of different styles on both fiddle and guitar. His hundreds of records include jazz, sloppy ballads, some of the most inventive guitar solos ever made, superlative and influential duets with white guitarist Eddie Lang, silly nonsense songs, and blues of considerable social comment. His voice was sweet and swarmy – nothing threatening in even his bitterest numbers.

Johnson acted as house guitarist for Okeh, accompanying numerous singers of varying merit. He also joined Louis Armstrong and Duke Ellington on occasion, providing guitar breaks of dazzling virtuosity far beyond the imagination of most blues singers. Apart from a break in the 1930s, he recorded almost continuously through to the end of the 1960s – a longer active career than any other bluesman.

Many of the St Louis bluesman were discovered by

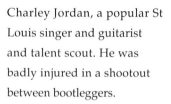

Charley Jordan, a popular St
Louis singer and guitarist
and talent scout. He was
badly injured in a shootout
between bootleggers.

Jesse Johnson, a black record distributor and talent scout.
Most had moved up from the South, including Henry
Townsend from Shelby, Mississippi, who had a long and
fruitful career recording under his own name and as a
backing guitarist for most of the big selling 1930s' stars;
Charley Jordan, a sour-voiced bootlegger and talent
scout, whose guitar style betrayed his country origins;
'Hi' Henry Brown, a very competent but little-recorded
Mississippi singer with an interesting, gravelly voice;
and J. D. 'Jelly Jaw' Short, a primitive Mississippi bluesman who played his guitar in an old-fashioned flailing
style. Unsubtle perhaps, but tremendously exciting.

Exciting was not a word associated with Peetie
Wheatstraw, the 'Devil's Son-in-Law' and the 'High
Sheriff of Hell', a heavily recorded pianist with a
slurred delivery who repeated the same theme endlessly
and whose popularity and influence, many collectors
feel, blighted blues through to the 1950s. Some of his
non-format records were excellent; 'Throw Me in the
Alley' with a gutbucket band, for instance, is a knockout,
as are his various stomps.

Another ex-Mississippi player was Blind Teddy
Darby, who made some memorable sides for Paramount

before settling into more routine material. There were
plenty of good pianists, too, like Wesley Wallace,
Sylvester Palmer, Henry Brown (not Hi Henry, the
guitarist), the heavy-voiced 'Barrel House' Buck
McFarland, and Aaron Sparks. James 'Stump' Johnson,
Walter Davis and Roosevelt Sykes were based in St
Louis, as were travelling bluesman Big Joe Williams
from Mississippi, Clifford Gibson from Louisville,
Kentucky, and Sylvester Weaver, who recorded the first
two country blues instrumentals back in 1923.

St Louis was also a big centre for women singers, with
a distinct, squeezed nasal sound which is hard to enjoy
these days. The most important included 'Signifying'
Mary Johnson and Little Alice Moore.

The piano was an important instrument in city clubs
and bars. There seems little doubt that the piano blues
started, in its original form, in the melting pot of New
Orleans in the days that Jelly Roll Morton evoked so
effectively. It may have developed away from ragtime
in the labour camps of Texas and Louisiana.

Some blues pianists followed the road North, others
stayed down South entertaining workers in logging
camps, bars, on the levees (the banks built to keep the

Mississippi from overflowing) and tiny barrelhouse joints (drink was sold direct from barrels), which gave the rougher end of the piano blues its name.

There were hundreds of these anonymous pianists wandering across the South, and few were recorded. The only memorial they have is a list drawn from the memory of Little Brother Montgomery, a first-rate, sensitive pianist and singer who did record extensively, and who remembered unsung heroes like Rip Top, Papa Lord God,

Roosevelt Sykes (left), 'The Honeydripper', who recorded for more than 50 years and left a huge collection of wonderful (and not so wonderful) piano blues.

Little Brother Montgomery (below), one of the great blues pianists and the source of much information on the history of the music.

Vocal with Piano

BLACK EVIL BLUES
(MOORE)

ALICE MOORE
(Little Alice from St. Louis)

7028 A

Flunkey Johnson, Ragging Willie Wells, Skinny Head Pete, Burnt Face Jake and Stiff Arm Eddie. 'Them guys were great piano players', he recalled.

Some blues pianists pre-empted the avant-garde experimentation of John Cage and Keith Tippett by putting tacks in the hammers to give a more metallic, percussive sound. Most preferred the added coloration of an old upright with the front off.

If, as Roy Carew said so memorably, boogie woogie was the bad boy of the rag family, did the boogie rhythm originate with banjo rhythms, or was it a piano style adopted by numerous guitarists? Was it derived from novelty effects used by vaudeville pianists to imitate a train or a moving horse? No one is too sure but the first mention of boogie woogie on record was as late as 1928 in 'Pine Top's Boogie Woogie' by Clarence 'Pine Top' Smith, a record which successfully fused the old-style walking bass (also found in a lot of guitar blues) with variations in the treble.

It was an important record which probably led to a lot more obscure pianists being recorded than might otherwise have happened. Interestingly, the lyrics suggest the boogie woogie was a dance, just another facet of the blues. Some of the bass figures Pine Top used appear in 'The Rocks' by Clay Custer, recorded in 1923, which suggest boogie woogie was an established style just waiting for a name. Cow Cow Davenport, a fine player himself whose rolling 'Cow Cow Blues' was adopted by many other pianists and guitarists, claims to have invented

the name in 1924, although a boogie was a nickname for a house rent party in Chicago.

But most of the pianists who did record (and often turned out records of far greater technical skill than their guitarist counterparts) are biographical blanks. Pine Top Smith came from Alabama, toured with travelling shows as a singer, dancer and comedian, was recommended to Brunswick-Vocalion by Cow Cow Davenport, and was shot in 1929 in a dance hall brawl after recording just eight numbers. But what about Charles Avery, whose one issued side is a storming boogie, Bob Call, Raymond Barrow, Rudy Foster, Leroy Garnett or Jabo Williams? All are mysteries, apart from an occasional half-remembered memory which may refer to other players anyway. At least one photo exists of Jabo, as well as a few worn 78s, which is more than can be said for most of the others.

Better known to history was Charlie Spand, possibly from Georgia, who turned out a highly praised duet with Blind Blake called 'Hastings Street', as well as a legacy of fine boogies and blues. Cow Cow Davenport recorded a number of dreary vaudeville sides and accompanied some very forgettable singers, but his own output mixes ragtime, boogie and stride piano with enormous exuberance.

Romeo Nelson and Montana Taylor both recorded a small number of the finest quality boogies, so good that it seems extraordinary that they weren't offered more sessions. And there was Cripple Clarence Lofton, up from Tennessee and an out-and-out entertainer, whose 'Streamline Train' (influenced by 'Cow Cow Blues') was one of the best railroad pieces ever recorded. 'Strut That Thing', another of his showcases, featured finger-snapping and rip-roaring instrumental breaks between the slick jive lyrics. Luckily, Lofton was recorded extensively until union problems cut short his recording career in the 1950s.

Louise Johnson, a friend of Son House and Charley Patton, made four sides in 1930, which many listeners believed had Lofton on piano because of the similarities in style. Son House, however, insisted Louise played herself, and the recordings are four youthful and aggressive gems.

Charley Taylor, an associate of Ishmon Bracey, came from Louisiana, but his style echoed that of the Texas pianists. A more curious case was Meade Lux Lewis, who recorded the highly influential and popular 'Honky Tonk Train Blues' for Paramount in 1927, and then

Jimmy Yancey, discovered by collectors after other pianists praised his boogie and blues piano playing. He made a wealth of fine recordings.

nothing else apart from accompaniments until 1935.

But there were so many others, from the widely recorded Roosevelt Sykes, Jimmy Yancey and the rag-influenced Will Ezell, to unknowns like Bert M. Mays, Lonnie Clark, Barrel House Welch (who even recorded with Louis Armstrong), Turner Parrish and Freddie Brown, who are little more than names on records.

By 1930, however, there was a growing demand for new blues, rather than repetitions of the old ones. Like the music-hall artists in Britain, who could use the same limited act everywhere they went until radio and film arrived, blues singers who simply recycled traditional verses soon ran out of material when they recorded.

Blind Lemon Jefferson kept going because he had a

real talent for composing new songs, and even his last sessions contain some very original material. The same went for groups like the Mississippi Sheiks and the jug bands, whose material was wide and varied enough to stave off boredom. It is interesting to speculate what might have happened, which artists might have gone on to adapt their styles to changing tastes if, in 1929, the first golden years of blues recording had not been cut short by the Depression.

The great American Depression, which started with the Wall Street Crash of 1929, was one of the worst disasters, apart from war, to face any modern country. Everyone, rich and poor, was affected, as banks collapsed, savings were wiped out and a quarter of the entire labour force lost their jobs. For the first time, many ordinary, hard-working Americans were forced to turn to breadlines and soup kitchens or starve, and there was an enormous increase in the number of travellers looking everywhere for work. By 1932, more than 5,500 banks and more than 100,000 other businesses had gone bust, and those in work faced wage cuts and shorter working hours. By 1933, 12 million people were out of work.

The Depression was caused by a startling imbalance between the rich and the poor. Twelve million families, some 42 per cent of the population, were barely on subsistence level, and many rural homes had neither running water nor electricity. Yet statistics show that the 36,000 richest families had a greater income than all 12 million put together, and while wages went up by 11 per cent, profits and dividends rose by 60 per cent. Such a narrow concentration of wealth meant factories were turning out more goods than anyone could afford to buy, and a decline in world trade added to the problems.

Needless to say, the black population – already at the bottom of the heap – felt the effects of the crash worst. At least they would have, had they had anything to lose, as Georgia Tom Dorsey commented in an interview with the BBC: 'I don't know what brought on the Depression. I didn't feel so depressed for I didn't have a thing to start with.'

At least the weather down South was warmer, and thousands of blacks headed sadly back home. Those who stayed faced ferocious rent increases which at least gave employment to the bluesmen hired to raise the money at rent parties.

The record companies ran into serious problems.

Paramount managed to keep going because of its low production costs and even tried out a few new artists like guitarist Marshall Owens from Birmingham, Alabama, and King Solomon Hill. But by 1932 the end was inevitable.

There was a final session for Blind Blake and Jabo Williams, and a full 21-song session by the Mississippi Sheiks, whose big hit 'Sittin' on Top of the World', had been made two years earlier. Only 12 of the songs were issued (the existence of the others is suggested only by missing matrix numbers) and the Sheiks were paid

Blind Joe Reynolds was given a chance to record for Paramount in 1929 after a talent scout felt sorry for him. He didn't sell but collectors would pay a fortune for his one undiscovered 78.

just $250. In their heyday on Okeh they received $1,000 a day.

Paramount finally folded in late 1933, although no one noticed. By the time Decca, a new company, realized what had happened and tried to buy the Paramount catalogue, all the metal masters, including dozens of unissued sides had been sold to a junk dealer and were lost for ever.

Many Paramounts survive as just one or two barely audible copies, but 35 have never been found by collectors including long sought-after couplings by Blind Joe Reynolds, J. D. Short, Big Bill Broonzy, Son House, Henry Townsend, Blind Blake, King Solomon Hill, Marshall Owens and Bumble Bee Slim. There may be more treasures still undiscovered; no one even knows what was on eight of the missing 35, which are simply catalogue numbers.

A remarkable pile of Paramount test pressings was found by pure luck in 1986 and included unissued songs or takes by singers as important as Son House, Charley Patton and Charlie Spand. The last missing Paramount by Blind Roosevelt Graves was finally found in the early 1990s, as was an unknown Curley Weaver previously credited to Clifford Gibson. Some of the others may still be recovered, but the chances grow less each year.

The record industry had had a boom year in 1927, with sales (for all kinds of music) exceeding $100 million. The following year Vocalion signed up Leroy

Carr, a likeable singer and pianist whose 'How Long, How Long Blues' was as influential and much copied as Jim Jackson's earlier 'Kansas City Blues'.

Vocalion also had a giant hit of another kind with Georgia Tom and 'Guitar Wizard' Tampa Red singing a mildly salacious little song called 'It's Tight Like That', which started a craze for hokum-style soundalikes (Paramount even started a group called the Hokum Boys, which occasionally included Tom and Tampa). Hokum was amazingly popular for such a limited style, and everyone from Blind Willie McTell to Lonnie Johnson had a 'Tight Like That' variation in their repertoire.

But even new stars Leroy Carr (10 records in 1929) and the popular Tampa Red (17 records) could not stave off the disaster which was rapidly looming. Figures researched by discographer Dan Mahoney show that the average number of copies of each new blues and gospel record issued by Columbia fell from 11,000 in 1927 to 1,000 by the end of 1930. Only 350 to 400 were pressed of each of the last 22 in their 14000 race series, and Columbia couldn't even sell these.

The Starr Piano Company killed their Gennett label, which had recorded Cryin' Sam Collins, William Harris and Cow Cow Davenport, among others, but struggled on with the cheaper Champion and Superior subsidiaries until 1934, when the group folded.

The fortunes of the record companies reflect the turbulent times and the rapidly changing ownership of all kinds of businesses. Columbia had merged with Okeh in 1926, and was taken over in 1931 by Grimsby-Grunow, which folded in 1934. It was then bought by Brunswick Record Corporation (BRC), a sister company of the America Record (ARC) conglomerate, formed by the merger of Plaza, Pathé and Cameo in 1929.

Consolidated Film Industries owned both ARC and BRC, and added Brunswick, Melotone and Vocalion to the roster in 1931, before snapping up Columbia–Okeh to make a very powerful group. Ironically, ARC and BRC were bought by Columbia Broadcasting System (CBS) in 1938 and again became Columbia Recording Corporation.

By 1931, even Bessie Smith, Barbecue Bob and guitar evangelist Blind Willie Johnson were finding it hard to sell more than a few hundred records. Johnson's sales had remained steady as the Depression bit, and he had seven records issued in 1930, but even the consolations of religion didn't count when there was no money. Columbia had no new artists to offer.

The Mississippi Sheiks were still selling reasonably

Sam Chatmon, last survivor
of the amazing musical Chatmon
family which also included
Charley Patton and Bo Carter.
He was also a member of the
Mississippi Sheiks.

Columbia 14000 series after 681 releases over nine years. Columbia recorded little in 1933, apart from the Sheiks and Bessie Smith – the latter a final session for the 'Empress of the Blues' at the request of the English Parlophone label, rather than for the American race market.

ARC tackled the Depression by keeping record prices low, and used mainly popular artists singing modern material. Some of it was of high quality; sides by the Famous Hokum Boys, featuring Georgia Tom and Big Bill Broonzy, had an affable, raffish charm, and a stack of sides (largely unissued) were made by Cryin' Sam Collins. They renamed him Salty Dog Sam, claimed he was 'just in from the South' and told dealers, 'A down-home record by a down-home artist. Be sure to demonstrate this record to every Negro that comes to your counter. Tell them its made by a real Negro.'

They were good sides, in Sam's high voice and slightly out-of-tune guitar, and included a version of 'Sitting on Top of the World'. So did a set by the Two Poor Boys, an Alabama duo obviously aimed at the same market as the Sheiks, who had themselves already made 'Sitting on Top of the World No. 2' and several similar variations on the theme.

By 1930 BRC dominated the market with acts who would become the stars of the 1930s: Tampa Red, Leroy Carr and Memphis Minnie. When BRC joined with ARC they gained Big Bill Broonzy too.

Victor managed to get through the Depression without merger or collapse, but in 1931 cut blues and gospel releases from 120 a year to around 40. There were a few field trips, but many Victor releases were songs recorded a few years earlier but not then released. Victor records were still expensive, so in 1933 the company introduced one of the most famous blues labels of all – Bluebird – at a cheap price. Engineers were also urged to make the fullest use of studio time. Victor, which once averaged eight titles a day, recorded 35 on one day in 1933, while in 1936 pianist Little Brother Montgomery recorded 18 solo songs and instrumentals plus six accompaniments to Annie Turner and ex-Mississippi Sheik Walter Vincson in one marathon session. The quality of Montgomery's sides was remarkably high, despite such pressure, and they are records much sought after by collectors.

But sales figures for Victor's blues issues in the Depression years make aptly depressing reading: 765 for a Memphis Jug Band coupling; 473 for Kokomo Arnold's debut as Gitfiddle Jim on one of the fastest slide-guitar

well for Okeh, which also issued solo records by Bo Carter, a member of the famous Chatmon family, and a leading Sheik. They were simple, bawdy blues with strong guitar accompaniment, but seemed to suit the mood of the times. There was one last field trip to Atlanta in 1931 when they recorded Blind Sammie for Columbia and Georgia Bill for Okeh. Both names were pseudonyms for Blind Willie McTell.

In 1932 new owners Grimsby-Grunow ended the famous

spectaculars ever recorded: 391 for J. D. Short pretending to be R. T. Hanen; 262 for Blind Teddy Darby; 109 for an Oscar Woods–Ed Chafer duet (not surprisingly, no copy has yet been found by collectors); 77 for a Charley Jordan issue; and only 69 for a Kid Coley.

By 1934, of the dozens of companies who had been involved in blues recording before the Depression, only the ARC–BRC group and Victor were still functioning. They were joined that year by a newcomer, Decca, which was an offshoot of the English company. Decca's blues talent scout was Mayo Williams, the black recording manager who set Paramount on the road to success.

There were a few memorable blues inspired by the Depression. Tampa Red turned in a 'Depression Blues' in 1931, and Joe Stone (J. D. Short under yet another *nom-de-disque*) recorded a dynamic 'It's Hard Time', which mentioned Hoovervilles, the shanty towns set up by homeless wanderers and sarcastically named after President Hoover, who was said to be more concerned with helping businesses recover than with aiding the unemployed.

Peg Leg Howell sang about how the rolling mill had closed down, and Barbecue Bob about the problems facing the homeless when winter arrived ('Cold Wave Blues'). Lonnie Johnson echoed Georgia Tom's view of the Depression in his 'Hard Times Ain't Gone Nowhere', when he sang, 'Hard times don't worry me, I was broke when they first started out'.

But perhaps the greatest of the Depression blues was Bessie Smith's 'Nobody Knows You When You're Down and Out'. It was recorded in 1929 before the full effects were felt but, like Bing Crosby's moving 'Buddy Can You Spare a Dime?' or the showstopping 'My Forgotten Man', from the Busby Berkeley film *Gold Diggers of 1933*, it spoke for millions who saw the hopes of the 1920s and the promises of a better life after the First World War melting like snow.

When Hoover lost the 1932 election to Franklin D. Roosevelt, the mood of America began to change as the new president promised a 'New Deal'. He set up various work agencies to revive industry and agriculture, and distribute the relief which Hoover had claimed would simply sap the will to work. The New Deal didn't do much for blacks, who were still no better off generally, but it inspired dozens of blues.

Some were bitter, like Carl Martin's 'Let's Have a New Deal', which attacked the reluctance of officials to help black people, or Walter Roland's 'Red Cross Store', which spoke of the humiliation of having to queue for charity. Jack Kelly and his South Memphis Jug Band put out a tribute to Roosevelt's enthusiastic energy in 'President Blues', while Speckled Red sang about the help available in 'Welfare Blues'.

Other singers turned their attention to various aspects of the New Deal, like the Public Works Administration (PWA), and the Civil Works Administration (CWA).

The CWA tried to help the 19 million unemployed in 1934 with work projects, ranging from digging drains to building up the river levees. Walter Roland seemed a bit happier about that in his 'CWA Blues' than he had been with the 'Red Cross Store', while Jimmy Gordon begged the president to keep up the good work in 'Don't Take Away My PWA', as did the Mississippi Mudder (Charlie McCoy) in 'Charity Blues'. Casey Bill Weldon had a fine 'WPA Blues', while Peetie Wheatstraw sang about 'Working on the Project'.

When Roosevelt died suddenly in 1945, there were plenty of blues tributes to what he had tried to do, including Champion Jack Dupree's 'FDR Blues', Big Joe Williams's 'His Spirit Lives On' and James McCain's 'Good Mr Roosevelt'.

As the USA struggled to rebuild itself, so did the small part of the record industry that recorded race music. But emerging from the bleak years was a different sort of blues, and one which owed more to the tough street of the city ghettos than the backwoods.

4
Rag, Mama, Rag

Into the Cities

Between 1927 and 1932 overall record sales dropped
from 104 million to a mere 6 million. Field recordings were reduced to a handful (Memphis was ignored
completely from 1931–1939), which meant that unknown
performers who might have been given a try-out on a
tune or two had no openings. The emphasis turned away
from the country and into the city, and regional styles
began to merge into a blander, more homogenous style.
That's a generalization, of course and there were still
records made by regional performers in a regional style,
both commercially and by the Library of Congress,
which sent out teams around the country to preserve the
USA's folk music before it was too late.

Much commercial recording was based in Chicago, and
there is no doubt that many of the most recorded singers
developed a routine and often repetitive style. This was
hardly surprising. Peetie Wheatstraw, for instance,

Big Bill Broonzy, once
thought to be the last of the
old time country bluesman,
but in reality a gifted and
sophisticated performer in
styles ranging from ragtime
to Chicago. One of the first
blues singers to visit Europe.

recorded more than 160 sides under his own name between a fine duet with (possibly) J. D. Short in 1930 to his death in 1941, often in sessions of eight songs or more. He was immensely popular and many of his blues are lyrically interesting, but heard one after another (as was never intended in the days before LPs), they become repetitive. Yet who can deny the appeal of a man whose colleagues gave themselves nicknames which reflected some of his glory: Peetie Wheatstraw's Brother (Jimmie Gordon), Peetie's Boy (Robert Lee McCoy), Peetie Wheatstraw's Buddy (Harmon Ray), and the Devil's Daddy-in-Law (Floyd Council).

Chicago in the 1930s was a rough and violent place, with black families squeezed into tiny apartments, often shared on the 'hot-bed' principle, where each family would get bed and room for eight hours. But there were speakeasies, bootleg liquor clubs and rent parties and, after Prohibition was repealed in 1933 the club market opened up. For the first time the blues had stars who were based in Chicago and St Louis, but who took their shows on the road.

A vital figure on the Chicago blues scene was Lester Melrose, a white music publisher, who had been involved in the 1920s' jazz market, and with the Gennett and Vocalion labels. By 1934 he sensed the changes that were happening in black music, and the new opportunities. In a revealing interview in *American Folk Music Occasional* in 1970 Melrose recalled:

> *In February of 1934 taverns were opening up and nearly all of them had juke boxes for entertainment. I sent a letter, which was just a feeler, to both RCA Victor and Columbia Records, explaining that I had certain blues talent ready to record and that I could locate any amount of relevant blues talent to meet their demands. They responded at once with telegrams and long-distance phone calls.*
>
> *From March 1934 to February 1951 I recorded at least 90 per cent of the talent of all rhythm and blues talent for RCA Victor and Columbia.*
>
> *My record talent was obtained through just plain hard work. I used to visit clubs taverns and booze joints in and around Chicago; also I used to travel all through the Southern states in search of talent and sometimes I had very good luck. As a rule I had considerable trouble with plantation owners as they were afraid I would be the cause of their help refusing to return.*

Big Bill Broonzy, a Melrose entertainer, recalled one famous occasion when Melrose was trying to find Tommy McClennan, an eccentric, gravel-voiced singer on a plantation near Yazoo City. Melrose disregarded Bill's warnings that whites from the North were regarded with deep suspicion, and had to run, leaving his car behind. McClennan and his friend Robert Petway did eventually record for Bluebird, and their rich, Mississippi blues, sung with voices as rough as Charley Patton's, had changed little from a decade before.

Big Bill had first recorded a decade before, too, but his style had changed dramatically. He had moved to Chicago from Arkansas in 1920, and had approached Mayo Williams at Paramount to see if he could record. Williams told him to go away and practise, and he made his first records for Paramount in 1927 with the unknown John Thomas. In the next few years he recorded widely as Sammy Sampson, Big Bill Johnson, Big Bill Broomsley and, eventually just as Big Bill.

His early records were infectious ragtime numbers, including some flat-pick showcases like 'How Do You Want It Done?', which he learnt from an older singer, Louis Lasky, who sadly recorded little. Bill was a member of the Chicago Black Swans, the Famous Hokum Boys, the Midnight Ramblers, the State Street Boys, the State Street Swingers, and even the Chicago Sanctified Singers, as well as backing countless others from Papa Charlie Jackson to Sonny Boy Williamson.

His 1930s' records settled into a more predictable groove, but he varied his backings from just guitar, piano and bass up to a small band called the Memphis Five, which echoed the jazz-blues hybrid of the Harlem Hamfats or Tampa Red's Chicago Five.

In many ways, listening to Big Bill's records in chronological order is a good way to hear the development of the blues, from the light country stomps and hokum numbers to the heavier beat provided by a drummer, which eventually led to the electric Chicago blues of the early 1950s.

Tampa Red (born Hudson Woodbridge) also started with a country sound. He went to Chicago from Tampa, Florida, where he had been brought up by his grandparents, whose name, Whittaker, he eventually adopted. In Chicago he teamed up with Georgia Tom Dorsey, although his first record, for Paramount, was a rather ordinary 'Through Train Blues'.

Red and Tom became part of a jug band backing Ma Rainey, but their first record as a duo, 'It's Tight Like

He played with Ma Rainey in the twenties. Tampa Red, The Guitar Wizard, was a towering figure in the blues for more than 40 years.

That', was a staggering hit. It was a jaunty little non-sense song, but it caught on in a big way and spawned numerous copies. They recorded it again the next month, with the suggestive vocals of female impersonator Frankie Jaxon making it sound even dirtier.

'It's Tight Like That No. 2', and 'No. 3' followed, as did a solo guitar version by Tampa, which emphasized the limitations of the tune. The duo even accompanied an unknown singer called Papa Too Sweet on yet another version, while they recorded endless variations them-selves as the Hokum Boys.

Like Bill Broonzy, Tampa Red was also called on as a house guitarist for many singers, and he made numerous enjoyable records, both solo and with Georgia Tom. He was a superb slide player, concentrating on the upper strings, and was known justly as the Guitar Wizard.

Again like Broonzy, he was able to adapt to changing styles. When Georgia Tom gave up blues for the church in 1932, Tampa moved on and turned out dozens of blues, pop and jazz numbers in a career that lasted until 1960 and in which he recorded more than 360 titles. In fact, his career shows how short the history of the blues has really been. He started recording with Ma Rainey in the era of Classic blues and lasted long enough to work with Johnnie Jones, pianist with one of the most important post-war singers, Elmore James.

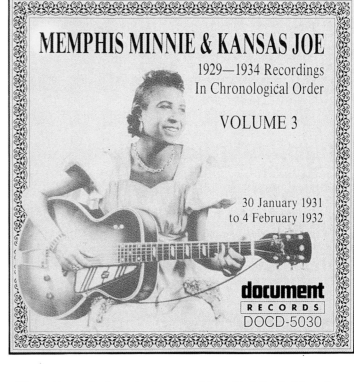

The guitar and piano duets of Scrapper Blackwell and Leroy Carr (left) sold thousands of records in the thirties, including the phenomenally popular 'How Long How Long Blues'.

Memphis Minnie (above), the best female blues singer of the lot, made a dazzling run of duets with her then husband, Joe McCoy. She adapted her style to changing tastes and was even part of the post-war Chicago scene.

Leroy Carr, another of the major 1930s' stars, came from Indianapolis, the Naptown of one of his blues, and usually recorded with the brilliant guitarist Scrapper Blackwell. He was a quiet, subtle singer with a wistful quality, which can be heard on his first record, 'How Long, How Long Blues', from 1928. It was a huge hit and led to at least five new versions by Carr alone. It is a beautiful record sung in Carr's warm and touching manner, with a gentle piano accompaniment punctuated by Blackwell's tense, plangent guitar.

They were a superb partnership and many of their records such as 'Blues Before Sunrise' and 'When the Sun Goes Down', are enduring classics. But they could romp too with all the drive of the best barrelhouse numbers, and there was also room for unusual novelty numbers like the seemingly autobiographical 'Carried Water for the Elephants', 'Papa Wants a Cookie' or 'Getting All Wet'.

Carr died suddenly in 1935 of nephritis from acute alcoholism, and Scrapper Blackwell was one of several to pay him tribute on record with 'My Old Pal Blues'.

Bill Gaither, a Louisville record shop owner with a similar kind of voice, even recorded as Leroy's Buddy, although he had to use Honey Hill as pianist. His first record (of more than 100) was 'Naptown Stomp'.

The other big star of the 1930s was a woman, Memphis Minnie, one of the finest blues singers and guitarists on record, regardless of sex. She was born in Louisiana but moved near Memphis in her childhood, and was playing on the streets of the city by the age of 15 as Kid Douglas. She travelled with a circus for several years and lived with Will Weldon of the Memphis Jug Band, before teaming up with Joe McCoy. There were heard by a talent scout performing in a barber shop in Beale Street, and travelled to New York to record six titles, three with Joe on vocal, including his famous Mississippi flood song, 'When the Levee Breaks'.

One of the songs, not issued immediately, was 'Bumble Bee', a suggestive but scarcely innovative number. Six months later Minnie and Joe made a new version for a Vocalion field recording unit, and it was so successful that Columbia hurriedly issued theirs. Victor promptly borrowed Minnie to make a third version as lead singer with the Memphis Jug Band, to which Vocalion responded with 'Bumble Bee No. 2' and 'New Bumble Bee'.

The duets made by Minnie and Joe from 1929 to 1934 when they broke up, rank with Stokes and Sane or Garfield Akers and Joe Callicott as the epitome of the Memphis two-guitar sound. One would take the lead, weaving dazzling patterns of arpeggios and ornamentation around the perfectly matched bass line of the other. The extent of their musical imagination coupled with their technical skills and their intuitive awareness of each other made for music of great beauty and power – power which remains undimmed on their records 60 years later. Even the simple call-and-answer hokum numbers they often recorded took on a new depth in their hands, for the empathy between them was astonishing.

Both recorded solo as well, but Joe was a fairly dull singer, and his best early work, apart from the odd classic like 'Evil Devil Woman', is undoubtedly in the context of the duets. Minnie, however, was a major artist in whatever setting she chose.

After they broke up, Joe produced some excellent updated country blues like 'Well, Well', became sanctified as Hallelujah Joe, and ran a washboard band with Robert Lee McCoy (or McCollum) and his own brother, Charlie. He was also Hamfat Ham, the main vocalist in the Harlem Hamfats, best of all the Chicago bands that united jazz with blues, in which Charlie also played.

Minnie stayed in the blues idiom, despite one gospel venture as Gospel Minnie, changing her style in the mid-1930s away from the rural Memphis sound to the tougher, new small band Chicago style. She carried on playing the clubs and recording with her then husband, Little Son Joe (and updating her style) until the early 1950s, and even appeared on the most important new Chicago label, Chess, before a stroke ended her long and active career. She died in 1973, her sad last years eased by blues fans from all over the world, who sent her cash and gifts after an appeal by Chris Strachwitz of Arhoolie Records, who reissued some of the best of her 180-plus issued sides to raise money for her.

At least she was never forgotten, as so many of her contemporaries were, and that says a lot for her lasting appeal. It seems apt that her biography by Paul and Beth Garon, *Woman with Guitar*, may be the best book ever written on one blues performer.

Pianist Sammy Price (above) who backed dozens of blues artists in the thirties and made numerous fine jazz records.

Joe McCoy (below), one time husband of Memphis Minnie and a lesser star in his own right. He played country blues, shouted gospel and fronted the Harlem Hamfats jazz-blues fusion band.

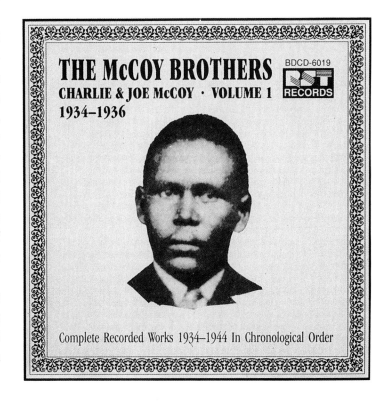

THE McCOY BROTHERS
CHARLIE & JOE McCOY · VOLUME 1
1934–1936
BDCD-6019
RST RECORDS
Complete Recorded Works 1934–1944 In Chronological Order

There were many other blues singers who recorded extensively in the 1930s. Georgia White was a delightful singer-pianist who started her career with Jimmy Noone's Apex Club Orchestra before turning out some interesting city blues for Decca, including 'The Blues Ain't Nothing But', a really great update of the old barrelhouse stomps.

There was Lucille Bogan (aka Bessie Jackson), who had started her career in 1923 on one side of the first race record made on location, and who recorded heavily until 1935 when she disappeared. She had a rough-edged, unsophisticated voice, and her blues were fairly grim and bleak. To her goes the credit of recording one of the few unexpurgated blues which have survived from the pre-war years, with the exception of Jelly Roll Morton's Library of Congress sides, which preserved some of the bawdy New Orleans songs recorded elsewhere with carefully edited lyrics.

In 1935 Bogan made a standard version of 'Shave 'Em Dry', a fairly innocuous song, it seemed, which Ma Rainey had also recorded back in 1924. But another version was also recorded at probably the same session, and this couldn't be more different. Bogan, who also sang about prostitution ('Tricks Ain't Walking No More') and lesbianism ('BD Woman Blues'), advertises what she has to offer in verses of increasing frankness and anatomical detail, which emphasize how bowdlerized the raunchier blues like 'The Dozens' and 'Sweet Jelly Rollin'' really were on record.

How this vastly enjoyable bit of eroticism came to be recorded isn't clear – possibly it was a private recording for the engineer – but its survival is a rare glimpse into a world of which records only hint. Other unexpurgated blues were recorded in the same way, but so far only one has been found.

When you couldn't be blatant, you had to be suggestive, as Lil Johnson, another Chicago entertainer who survived the Depression, showed with with her hymns to 'Hot Nuts (Get 'Em from the Peanut Man)' and invitations to 'Press My Button (Ring My Bell)' and 'Let's Get Drunk and Truck'.

Robert Lee McCoy, possibly the doomiest, gloomiest singer ever recorded, made a lot of sombre recordings, including a bottleneck classic in 'Friars Point Blues'. He went on with more Tampa Red-inspired records for Chess and United in the 1950s as Robert Nighthawk, never sounding anything but miserable.

Big Joe Williams, the archetypal wandering blues-

The archetype of the travelling bluesman, Big Joe Williams (left) spent his life wandering and playing his nine-string guitar. He recorded widely and rarely poorly, and was a major performer for around half a century.

Big Joe Williams recorded a song about Whistling Pines (right), located outside Crawford, Mississippi.

Walter Davis (left), a highly popular singer, pianist and lyric writer in the thirties, despite a tendency to use the same tune endlessly.

Sonny Boy Williamson No. 1 (above) who made the harmonica a lead instrument and wrote the ground rules for the new Chicago sound. A milestone musician.

man, also recorded a lot on a unique nine-string guitar which he adapted himself. An extraordinarily fast player, using flurries of notes to back his heavy voice, his records have an intensity and emotion which few of his contemporaries achieved. Joe recorded very heavily for collectors' labels after the war, but his best sides are the magnificent band numbers with Sonny Boy Williamson, made for Columbia in the late 1940s. (Williamson is not to be confused with the Sonny Boy who toured Europe in the 1960s, who was an equally talented singer and harmonica player named Aleck Rice Miller.)

The first Sonny Boy started recording in 1937, when he still had a very rural sound to his music, in a trio with Big Joe and Robert Lee McCoy. It was at this first session he made highly influential records like 'Good Morning, School Girl' and 'Blue Bird Blues', before moving on to the newer, heavier Chicago sound with piano, bass and, finally, drums. Many of his best records were waxed at Victor mega sessions; at one he played on 18 issued sides after pianist Walter Davis, who accompanied him on most of them, had already cut 18 solos of his own.

Williamson recorded with some of the best bluesmen

A sensitive study of veteran St Louis bluesman Henry Townsend and his wife Vernell (right).

William 'Jazz' Gillum (below), a popular singer and harmonica player in the thirties and forties.

in Chicago – guitarists Henry Townsend, Big Bill, Tampa Red and Charlie McCoy, mandolinists Yank Rachell and Willie Hatcher, pianists Speckled Red, Blind John Davis, Big Maceo, Eddie Boyd and Joshua Altheimer – and was immensely popular. He played superlative harmonica – indeed, made it part of the front line of a band rather than just a background accompaniment – and sang in a slurred, tongue-tied fashion which was much imitated and bridged the gap between the Chicago blues of the 1930s and the gutsier sound of Chicago in the 1950s.

His trademarks can be heard in many of the post-war country and city blues, but sadly he wasn't there to share in it. He was senselessly murdered with an icepick in 1948 and widely mourned.

Others who sold well at this time include William Jazz Gillum, a limited, pleasant singer and harmonica player whose earliest records feature country dance numbers of an earlier era. A better singer was Robert Brown (Washboard Sam), who claimed to be Big Bill's half-brother and who turned the washboard into a musical instrumental with a long series of records of great rhythmic drive, sung in one of the strongest blues voices of the Chicago era.

More restrained was Big Maceo Merriweather, a gentle singer with something of the yearning quality of Leroy Carr, but who could let rip like the best of the earlier boogie players in brilliant instrumentals like 'Chicago Breakdown' and 'Texas Stomp'. Sadly, he was crippled by a stroke in 1946, and his last records are shadows of his achievements at his peak.

Very different was Kokomo Arnold, a bootlegger and steel mill worker who played the Chicago clubs and bars, but wasn't keen to record. He played frenzied slide guitar, his instrument laid across his lap like Oscar Woods and Black Ace in Texas, and fretted with a glass. His first sides were the Gitfiddle Jim coupling mentioned earlier, which is now so rare that the album re-issue has been cobbled together from two damaged

copies. It was Kansas Joe McCoy who persuaded him, against his will, to record again for Decca. He was more interested in his moonshine business, but his first four sides in 1934 sold well.

One, 'Old Original Kokomo Blues', may have been inspired by Jabo Williams's 1932 record, 'Ko Ko Mo Blues', although Arnold himself told French writer Jacques Demetre that the phrase derived from a brand of coffee called Koko, to which he added another syllable for alliteration. 'Eleven Light City', the mysterious place to which the singer wants to go, turned out to be the name of a drugstore. No one seems to have confirmed this story or checked whether Koko coffee or the store existed, but the song was widely copied by dozens of other singers, including Robert Johnson on 'Sweet Home Chicago'.

The other side of the record was an even more copied song, 'Milk Cow Blues', which inspired numerous other blues on a cow or bull theme. It was a big hit and led Arnold to record virtually identical 'Milk Cow Blues' nos. 2–5, as well as several other songs using the same

Washboard Sam (Robert Brown), a superb singer (left), who made washboard playing an art on hundreds of records in the thirties and forties.

Kokomo Arnold, a brilliant slide guitarist whose best records are unrivalled for speed and accuracy. He recorded reluctantly and refused to take part in the sixties blues revival.

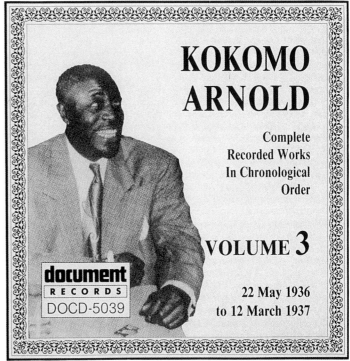

KOKOMO ARNOLD

Complete Recorded Works In Chronological Order

document RECORDS DOCD-5039

VOLUME 3

22 May 1936 to 12 March 1937

tune. But that first coupling is a *tour de force* by any standards, with some of the most stunning slide guitar ever recorded and rich, vibrant vocals. The song was also revived in the rock and roll era by Eddie Cochran and Elvis Presley. (Presley also used songs by Big Boy Crudup, Junior Parker and Smiley Lewis on his earliest recordings.)

Kokomo recorded regularly over the next four years, but most of his records degenerated into little more than reworkings of his earlier sides. There were a very few outstanding sides among the rehashes, but by 1938 it was over. Kokomo went back to his own quiet, anonymous life and refused to have anything to do with the blues revival in the 1960s. He died in 1968.

There were numerous other singers of varying merit. Jimmie Gordon, Red Nelson, Johnny Temple (his early records with Charlie McCoy revive that Memphis two-guitar sound to great effect). Merline Johnson, Bumble Bee Slim, Teddy Edwards, Champion Jack Dupree, Curtis Jones and Walter Roland all recorded extensively, although rarely memorably.

Merline Johnson (above), the Yas Yas Girl, shows off one of the dozens of records she made with jazz small groups in the thirties.

Champion Jack Dupree (right), Europe's favourite two fisted pianist.

His first records were pure Mississippi blues, but Arthur 'Big Boy' Crudup (left) became best known after Elvis Presley recorded some of his songs. A fine traditional performer who adapted to changing tastes but was more popular outside America.

Lil Green (below) started as one of the Bluebird roster and went on to make some solid R & B sides after the war. She died at the early age of 35.

Some collectors have termed the sound of the late 1930s as the Bluebird sound after the label on which so many similar-sounding records were issued. That description, however, is misleading. Bluebird also had the ferocious Tommy McClennan and Robert Petway, and the field-holler sound of the young Big Boy Crudup, among others, and Decca and Columbia turned out their fair share of dull and routine records too.

Perhaps the urban blues of the 1930s would be more accurately called the Melrose sound, as in his time Lester Melrose represented Big Bill, Washboard Sam, Tampa Red, Big Boy Crudup, Memphis Minnie, St Louis Jimmy Oden, Big Joe Williams, Leroy Carr, Sonny Boy Williamson, Tommy McClennan, Big Maceo, Bumble Bee Slim, Roosevelt Sykes, Walter Davis, Victoria Spivey, Jazz Gillum, Lil Green and Merline Johnson, among many others. Even so, there are quite a few variations in style among those performers.

5
On the Road Again
Back Down South

The growth of city blues didn't mean that country blues had died out. On the contrary, it was the record-buying public, largely city people, whose tastes had moved towards a more sophisticated sound. But the older forms of blues still survived, as Tommy McClennan and Big Boy Crudup demonstrated. In the East Coast states the record companies found plenty of singers and material for which there was still a demand.

In 1935 street musician Blind Boy Fuller (real name Fulton Allen) was heard in Durham, North Carolina, singing for tobacco workers by J. B. Long, a talent scout for the American Records Corporation (ARC). Extensive research by Bruce Bastin suggests Fuller learned much of his style from Gary Davis, another blind singer who was several years older, and who in turn was influenced by Willie Walker, a Greenville musician whom Davis reckoned was the best guitarist he had ever heard. Coming

Sonny Boy Williamson (II) delighted European audiences with his tremulous singing, down-home harmonica and remarkable two-tone suit and bowler. He is pictured here on the TV show, *Hullabaloo.*

BLIND BOY FULLER

Complete Recorded Works
In Chronological Order

VOL. 4
15 December 1937 to
29 October 1938

document
RECORDS
DOCD-5094

Blind Boy Fuller (Fulton
Allen) who learned much
from Gary Davis and perhaps

Buddy Moss too, and went on
to influence the sound of East
Coast blues himself.

from Davis, himself a dazzling guitarist, that is a real compliment.

Davis claimed to have taught Fuller much, and added caustically, 'He would have been all right if I kept him under me long enough'. Davis travelled with Fuller and George Washington, a washboard player who recorded as Oh Red, Bull City Red and Brother George, for a first session in New York.

Davis recorded first, producing only two blues before the war, and a superb coupling it was. Fuller's first tracks were good but Davis's were better, and it is no coincidence that the best records Fuller made at those earliest sessions had Gary Davis on second guitar. 'Rag Mama Rag', of which two takes happily survive, is a dance music masterpiece by any standard. Davis, however, refused to record any more blues and was, reluctantly, allowed to make some gospel records instead. They didn't sell, and Blind Gary's best musical years went unrecorded until white collectors rediscovered him in New York in 1945. He made one more single for the black market in 1949, then recorded steadily through the 1950s and 1960s, with few signs of age, until his death in 1972.

Fuller, however, was at the start of a good career, recording around 135 titles solo or with Red's wash-

board, sometimes with second guitar by Dipper Boy Council or Sonny Jones, or wailing harmonica by his new partner, Sonny Terry. He played the odd slide piece like 'Homesick and Lonesome', but mainly they were gritty, down-home blues, often fairly earthy, or jumping dance pieces. One of these, 'Truckin' My Blues Away', became a great favourite in the 1960s with Jefferson Airplane, among others.

Fuller's voice was coarse and unsubtle, his playing competent, with strong hints of Blind Blake, but with a much heavier approach. He died in 1940 after one last session with Sonny Terry and Oh Red at which they disguised themselves as Brother George and His Sanctified Singers for some religious numbers. Sonny Terry and Red later teamed up with Brownie McGhee, whom Long picked to replace his deceased star. He even had some of his early records issued as Blind Boy Fuller No. 2, despite the fact that their voices were very different.

McGhee and Terry stayed together for many years, and were the first real blues singers many young British fans saw in the post-war years. Sonny's unique harmonica playing and his eerie falsetto whoops and howls got him a place at the famous 1939 *Spirituals to Swing Concert* in Carnegie Hall, New York, and the two even

Jazz meets blues. Sonny Terry
(right) with partner Brownie
McGhee (left) and the great
jazz trumpeter Red Allen.

had a small spot playing in Tennessee Williams's *Cat on a Hot Tin Roof*. Both recorded heavily in the post-war years, in the new rhythm and blues style for their own people and as folk singers for the collectors' labels.

Others who modelled themselves on Fuller, for better or worse, included Dipper Boy Council (Blind Boy Fuller's Buddy) and Sonny Jones, who had actually recorded with him; brothers Richard (Little Boy Fuller) and Welly Trice, Roosevelt Antrim, Ralph Willis from Alabama and Carolina Slim.

Buddy Moss, who may have influenced Fuller almost as much as Gary Davis (he recorded in the so-called Fuller style two years before Fuller himself), had by now abandoned the hints of Barbecue Bob and Blind Blake heard on his earliest sessions.

By 1934, he was recording songs in a way which would soon become indelibly associated with Fuller. Perhaps it was a regional style, perhaps Moss heard Fuller play long before he recorded. The main difference was in the vocals – Fuller jaunty or grittily direct, Moss increasingly desolate and doomy. But Moss sold far better than his old friends Curley Weaver and Willie McTell and was asked back time and again.

In 1935, he was jailed for five years. He was released after pressure from his manager and recorded once more in 1941. Two months later, America was in the war, shellac was rationed and a recording ban imposed. Moss, one of the most talented of the East Coast group, gave up music until he was rediscovered in the sixties.

Other East Coast favourites included Josh White, who, in the 1940s, became more famous as a folk singer than a blues singer. He actually recorded heavily as Pinewood Tom and the Singing Christian, but his bland, uninvolved sound is, generally not to the liking of most modern collectors.

The Virginian Luke Jordan recorded 10 interesting sides in 1927, which seem to have sold well, although Jordan was never recorded again.

The medicine show duet, Pink Anderson and Blind Simmie Dooley, made just four very enjoyable, good-time tracks in 1928, and again were forgotten until Anderson resurfaced, still on top form, in 1950.

Other notables included Willie Walker's partner, Sam Brooks, who was almost as respected as Walker; minstrel show singer Lil McClintock, one of whose songs is a medley of pre-First World War tunes, complete with coon show chorus; and the magnificent Julius Daniels

Cousin Joe, or Pleasant Joseph, was a pianist with an irreverent sense of humour and deep growling voice. He often recorded with jazzmen like Mezz Mezzrow, Sidney Bechet and Dicky Wells.

from near Charlotte, South Carolina, whose 1927 records for Victor are delightfully sung and beautifully accompanied by two guitars.

As recording trips dried up, so did the discoveries. In 1936 Victor recorded dull pianist Peg Leg Ben Abney and the curious Cedar Creek Sheik, who may have been white but was certainly influenced by the medicine show style. More interesting was Virgil Childers, a complete unknown, who mixed Piedmont blues with, once again, songs from the travelling show tradition. Again, it is possible he was white.

Other finds included Kid Prince Moore, an eclectic singer-guitarist with a distinctly country feel about his rags and blues and Shorty Bob Parker, a harsh-voiced singer-pianist who accompanied him on some sides and whose own output includes lyrics lifted directly from a Lemon Jefferson song.

On the by-now rare trips to the South, Victor still managed to attract some interesting names. In New Orleans in 1936 it recorded Bo Carter, the Chatmon Brothers and Walter Jacobs (actually Walter Vincson) from the Mississippi Sheiks (the Sheiks as such had made their last record the previous year), plus Little

Sleepy John Estes (centre), is reunited with his old friends, mandolinist Yank Rachel (left) and harmonica player Hammie Nixon, after he was rediscovered, blind and in terrible poverty.

Brother Montgomery, Annie Turner and Creole George Guesnon in one marathon session, and Sonny Boy Nelson (Eugene Powell), a pleasant Mississippi bluesman, his wife Mississippi Matilda, and their friends Robert Hill and Willie Harris (Bo Carter was their agent).

There were some superb piano blues sessions in San Antonio in the following years, with memorable sides from Andy Boy, Walter 'Cowboy' Washington and Big Boy Knox. But apart from pianist Frank Tannehill and more Bo Carter, the few remaining Victor field trips concentrated on gospel.

Decca did one trip a year from 1936 to 1938, recording Walter Vincson again, plus Oscar Woods and Black Ace, and Texas pianists Black Ivory King, Blind Norris and Whistling Alex Moore. It also organized the first, unpromising, session by Andrew Hogg, who became very popular after the War as Smokey Hogg.

Decca also picked up one of the most unusual singers of all, Sleepy John Estes, who had previously recorded for a Victor field unit in Memphis. After making some unique sides with mandolinist Yank Rachel and pianist Jab Jones in which the three sometimes played simultaneously in three different tempi, Victor dropped him, and it was 1935, after he had moved to Chicago, before Decca tried him again.

Estes's eccentric style had changed a lot by then, becoming more strait-laced and conventional. He came from Brownsville, Tennessee, and was helped to develop his rudimentary guitar style by Hambone Willie Newbern, an older singer whose few recordings for Okeh included the earliest version of the 'Roll and Tumble' theme.

Estes sang in a curious crying style about matters of limited parochial interest and people he knew personally. Nearly all his blues were autobiographical; he was a singing newspaper, his pages always apparently on the point of disintegration but somehow hanging together until the end. He was joined on some records by Hammie Nixon, a harmonica player under the spell of Cannon's Jug Stompers, player Noah Lewis, or guitarists Son Bonds and Charlie Pickett.

Sleepy John recorded an unforgettable series of topical blues for Decca before returning briefly to Victor's Bluebird label with Bonds for a set of dance numbers as the Delta Boys. His last session was in 1941 – at least, collectors thought it was until unissued 1948 sides from the tiny Chicago Ora Nelle label came to light. Among them were two excellent Sleepy John sides. Since then, further records he made for Sun in 1952 have been discovered and issued although there is one complete session with Nixon which he made for the Bea and Baby label in Chicago in the 1950s which has never been heard.

To everyone's surprise (he always sounded so old, even when young), Sleepy John was rediscovered, blind and in terrible poverty, but still alive and well in the early 1960s, and his records for various collectors' labels showed little falling off in his powers. He even visited Europe with Hammie Nixon before his death in 1977.

Yank Rachel became friends with Sonny Boy Williamson and appeared as a sidesman on numerous Bluebird sessions, as well as making some forgettable sides for ARC and Victor under his own name. He, too, was recorded after the War. Son Bonds, who played the streets with Hammie Nixon, was a solid, gritty-voiced singer who made a series of reasonably interesting blues and gospel songs, although his reputation was always overshadowed by Estes. He was murdered, apparently by mistake, by a short-sighted gunman in 1947. Charlie Pickett is another biographical blank, who made four sides in a trembly, acidulous voice and then disappeared, unless, as some have suggested, he was the Dan Pickett who recorded after the War.

ARC were busier than most, although nothing like the heady days of the 1920s. In 1934 they picked up Leroy Carr, Scrapper Blackwell and Texas Alexander, while 1935 showed a rich yield from Texas and Jackson, Mississippi, including superb piano blues from Moaning Bernice Edwards, Black Boy Shine, Blind Mack, Kid Stormy Weather and Harry Chatmon. There were real backwoods country blues from Isaiah Nettles (the

Memphis Slim first recorded in the thirties and made hundreds of sides before his death in 1989. A strident singer and strong pianist, he managed to change his style with the times but many of his later recordings are forgettable.

THESAURUS OF CLASSIC JAZZ
ROBERT JOHNSON
KING OF THE DELTA BLUES SINGERS
COLUMBIA

'Mississippi Moaner') and the under-rated Willie Reed, and more sophisticated music from the Dallas Jamboree Jug Band, Funny Papa Smith, the original Howlin' Wolf (tragically all the recordings were found to be faulty), and Robert Wilkins (loosely disguised as Tim Wilkins).

Further treasures were collected on trips between 1936 and 1940, including Black Ace (B. K. Turner) and Oscar Woods again, who both played guitar across the lap with a glass slide to exciting effect. Texas pianists like Black Boy Shine, Son Becky, Pinetop Burks and Dusky Dailey also came to light, as did the final pre-war recordings of jug band veterans Jack Kelly and Charlie Burse (both surfaced briefly on the post-war Sun label), and Robert Johnson.

More has been written about Johnson than any other blues singer, largely because he has taken on an almost mythical quality. His lyrics suggest a tortured man driven by fear of the devil, a man who stood at the crossroads and sold his soul in exchange for extraordinary talents, a frightened man pursued by hell hounds. The first reissue of his records on LP did nothing to dispel this impression, as the man who recorded him recalled him as a petrified youngster who kept his back turned when he was playing.

What a surprise when a photograph of the great man was finally published in 1986! It showed an elegant young man in pinstripe suit, button-down shirt, waistcoat, polished shoes and jauntily tilted hat. All of a sudden, the hell hounds seemed more like lapdogs.

Johnson recorded just 29 tunes, plus alternate takes, and only eleven 78s were issued in his lifetime. Forty-one sides survive, and there are continual rumours of at least one more in the hands of a collector.

Johnson was the grandson of a slave and was born in Hazlehurst, Mississippi, in 1911. He was brought up in Robinsville, 40 miles south of Memphis, but was initially interested in playing the harmonica. He turned to the guitar in the late 1920s and got tips from Willie Brown, Charley Patton's old sidekick, and, occasionally, Patton himself. Son House later moved to Robinsville, becoming an even greater influence on the young player, and there is much of House's brooding intensity in Johnson's most powerful records.

He started wandering, playing small bars and drinking joints, entertaining work gangs and country parties, and being taught by unrecorded bluesman Ike Zinnerman. He learned well and practised hard, and in the following years travelled as far as Canada and New York from his base in Helena, Arkansas. It was here he met the great bluesmen of the time – some still to be recorded – like the second Sonny Boy Williamson (then called Little Boy Blue), Elmore James, David 'Honeyboy' Edwards, Howling Wolf, Johnny Shines and his own stepson, Robert 'Junior' Lockwood, to whom he taught much of his style. But, as mentioned before, his repertoire included every kind of music, as well as blues.

In 1936 Johnson contacted H. C. Speir, who had discovered so many major blues singers, and Speir arranged for him to record for ARC. His first session included a moderate hit, 'Terraplane Blues', and also 'I Believe I'll Dust My Broom', inspired by an early Kokomo Arnold record and later to become Elmore James's theme song.

Other sessions followed, including one on 27 November 1936 at which he recorded the sides on which his reputation with collectors is based – the almost hysterical 'Preaching Blues', the mystic 'Crossroads Blues', Son House's old 'Walking Blues' and the frenzied 'If I Had Possession Over Judgement Day', which echoed Willie Newbern's 'Roll and Tumble Blues'. Nothing that followed really approached this handful for sheer intensity and emotional involvement, which drove him to the point of incoherence. However, 'Stones in My Passway', 'Hellhound on My Trail' and 'Me and the Devil Blues' were all to add to the legends.

After a final session in June 1937, he never recorded again. By the time he was being chased to appear at the 1938 *Spirituals to Swing* concert, he was dead,

Johnny Shines (above left), a magnificent singer and guitarist whom success, sadly, eluded.

Robert Junior Lockwood (above right), Robert Johnson's stepson and a skilled, if unexciting, bluesman in own right.

David 'Honeyboy' Edwards (right), a friend of Robert Johnson recorded by the Library of Congress in 1942 but never really commercially successful. Still a powerful and individual performer.

Huddie 'Leadbelly' Ledbetter (opposite left), a one man archive of American folk song and a singer of unrivalled power and authority.

Son House (opposite right), one of the first generation of recorded Mississippi blues singers, and among the best. He recorded for Paramount and the Library of Congress and thrilled European fans with his archaic slide and hoarse vocals after his rediscovery in 1964.

Baby Boy Warren (left), a brilliant Detroit bluesman whose early fifties sides are much prized.

poisoned by, perhaps, a jealous husband. It was a short life but a fast one.

Many of Johnson's records were true originals; some were influenced by earlier singers, especially Lonnie Johnson on his dullest sides like 'Drunken Hearted Man', and, more fruitfully, Son House, the Mississippi Sheiks and Kokomo Arnold. But Johnson stood at the crossroads between the old and the new, the city and the country, and his handful of records was highly influential on many artists who came after him. Calvin Frazier, Johnny Shines, Robert Lockwood, Elmore James, Homesick James, Muddy Waters, Honeyboy Edwards, J. B. Hutto, Jimmy De Berry, Boyd Gilmore, Baby Face Leroy Foster, Baby Boy Warren, Big Joe Williams – all acknowledge a debt to Johnson who, like Charley Patton earlier, was there when the music needed him. Even the Rolling Stones paid tribute with an accurate version of 'Love in Vain'.

If Johnson stood at the junction of city and country blues, the real country blues were still being preserved by the Library of Congress (LOC) which, since 1933, had been sending out mobile recording units. They concentrated on prison farms and penitentiaries, rather than plantations, presumably because these places offered easier access to the singers. By 1942, the LOC teams had recorded more than 4,000 songs by 850 black singers, plus other sides with white country performers. Many of these have been reissued on LP and CD in recent years, giving some idea of the wealth of music in the archives. Sadly, the original acetates have deteriorated and many priceless originals are irretrievably damaged.

Many of the best recordings were made by John Lomax and his son Alan, who toured the South and whose efforts show how many top-notch artists the commercial companies missed. Particularly fine were the Texans Smith Casey and Pete Harris, Allison Mathis and Gus

Gibson from Georgia, and Lucious Curtis and Willie Ford from Mississippi, but there were numerous others of equally high standard.

The LOC caught a few who went on to make commercial records; Gabriel Brown, Buster Brown, Willie Blackwell, Calvin Frazier and Honeyboy Edwards come to mind, but there were a few who were, or became, giants in the field.

Huddie Ledbetter, a violent giant and a one-man storehouse of American folk song, was one of the greats. He was nicknamed Leadbelly, he came from Texas and he spent years in prison for assault and murder. He was discovered in the Louisiana State Penitentiary by the Lomaxes in 1933, and recorded hundreds of sides for the LOC in the next decade. His repertoire was vast, ranging across old field hollers, hymns, dance tunes, pop songs, country and western, ballads, topical songs, children's songs, lullabies and blues. It was his version of songs like 'Goodnight Irene', 'Rock Island Line', 'Take This Hammer', 'Pick a Bale of Cotton' and 'In the Pines' which became folk music standards all over the world. Indeed, without him, much of the music would have been lost.

Leadbelly played a 12-string guitar, occasionally with dramatic slide, with tremendous verve and his powerful singing always bordered on a shout. He knew Lemon Jefferson and from him picked up some songs and probably the ability to temper his power with a little subtlety, but Leadbelly was unique. There were more years in prison, recordings for commercial companies which never sold (he was probably too old-fashioned) and even a set with the a cappella Golden Gate Quartet. He became something of a symbol in New York in the 1940s, recording with Woody Guthrie, Cisco Houston, Sonny Terry and Brownie McGhee in a long series of sessions for the Folkways label.

The LOC also recorded Blind Willie McTell after his last pre-war commercial session, which included 'Hillbilly Willy's Blues', almost a parody of white country music. The Lomaxes seemed more interested in old songs and ballads than blues, so McTell duly obliged with a side of his repertoire that hadn't appeared on record before, plus fascinating anecdotes of his early years as an entertainer.

The recording unit found Son House twice, in 1941 and 1942, in Mississippi, and recorded him at length with

Willie Brown, plus Fiddlin' Joe Martin and Leroy Williams on mandolin and harmonica respectively. It's hard to say these records were influential because no one heard them, but the sheer power of the little band, with Son's fierce slide guitar balancing the heavy rhythm, was a strong hint of the way that Muddy Waters would lay down the ground rules for electric blues in the 1950s.

The songs were from the Delta, with echoes of Charley Patton throughout, but presented in a way that Patton might have developed had he lived. And, as if to emphasize once again how incomplete a picture records alone provide, Son also sang a curious song about the War called 'American Defense', which seemed to have its roots in white string band music, and a raggy number called 'Am I Right or Wrong'. There was also a strong version of Lemon Jefferson's 'See That My Grave Is Kept Clean' (renamed 'County Farm Blues'), which he had also recorded at his 1930 session, but which is among the missing Paramounts.

The LOC recordings allowed House to expand from the usual two- or three-minute limitation imposed by 78s, and the long 'Government Fleet Blues' with the band is among the best recordings Son ever made. He was rediscovered in the early 1960s and toured Europe, the oldest active survivor from the early days of the recorded Delta blues. On stage he was spellbinding. He was also recorded again, but none of his later records give much idea of the hypnotic power of his LOC sides, or the magnetism he generated in person.

The LOC team also visited Parchman, a notorious prison farm in Mississippi, where they found Booker ('Bukka' on record) White, who had first recorded two glorious train pieces with Napoleon Hairiston and two gospel sides with one Miss Minnie (possibly Memphis Minnie) in Memphis in 1930. Nothing came of them, but in 1937 he recorded again. One of the numbers was his own song, 'Shake 'Em on Down', which was very popular and recorded by numerous other singers, including Tommy McClennan and Big Joe Williams.

Booker White was jailed for murder before he could make any more sides, but he gave the Lomaxes two scorching bottleneck numbers, including a version of the perennial 'Poor Boy', which is as good as anything he ever did. Lester Melrose obtained his release from jail, and on two days in March 1940 he recorded 12 more titles of great power and lyrical honesty. The best known is 'Fixin' to Die, a heavily syncopated and doom-

ridden chant picked up by several white performers, but there are also several numbers which show how much the prison experience had affected him. They are highly personal, vividly developed and rank with the McClennan and House sides as the most durable country blues recorded at the end of the 1930s.

The Lomaxes' other great discovery was McKinley Morganfield, another Mississippi singer who, as Muddy Waters, became the unchallenged king of the Chicago blues in the 1950s. He recorded solo at first, a Son House-influenced 'Country Blues' and the jaunty 'I Be's Troubled'. He reworked both at his first recording session with the Chess brothers' Aristocrat label, and they were eagerly bought by homesick Southern families in Chicago.

Muddy also recorded with a little band led by Son Sims, a backwoods fiddler who had recorded with Charley Patton as Henry Sims. Like the Son House band tracks, these sides contained the embryo of the Chicago blues, while underlining the durability of the old Delta style.

The easy, loping boogie rhythm typified by Robert

Pinetop Perkins (right), who played for Sun Records and in Muddy Waters' band.

Bukka White (left), whose raw Mississippi sounds stood out from the formula blues of the late thirties. He was still in his prime when he was rediscovered and had a good second career in the blues revival.

Johnson adapted well to the new band sound which was developing at the beginning of the 1940s. It was a sound fed by the first radio blues shows, such as *King Biscuit Time* on a station based in Helena, Arkansas, which used Sonny Boy Williamson No. 2 and Robert Lockwood to help sell flour. It was immensely successful and the company even marketed a Sonny Boy White Corn Meal. Numerous other Southern singers took part in the show, including pianists Willie Love and Pinetop Perkins, and guitarists Houston Stackhouse and Joe Willie Wilkins. Other flour companies competed with gloomy Robert Nighthawk (Robert Lee McCoy), while Sonny Boy joined Elmore James to advertise a tonic.

Other radio stations tentatively scheduled blues record spots, and one Memphis station resisted pressure from white advertisers and gave itself over entirely to black music. It was a tremendous success and it meant that the music of those featured reached an even wider audience. It also created a demand for records hitherto issued by only a few major companies.

In 1942 the America Federation of Musicians called for a ban on recording, which its president James C. Petrillo claimed was killing live entertainment. There was also a shortage of shellac because of the War, and the big companies' interest in blues diminished.

It was the end of the Petrillo ban, the slow easing of wartime shortages and the demand for records by the radio stations that led to what has sometimes been called the second golden era of the blues.

6

Rollin' and Tumblin'

The Post-war Revival

The war years marked a watershed in blues recording. The big companies started cutting back on race records in 1941, although Decca claimed it had every blues issued since 1934 still in its catalogue. The number of new issues, however, fell dramatically, and was cut even further when the government restricted the use of shellac.

Victor's big sellers were Washboard Sam, followed by Tampa Red, Walter Davis, Sonny Boy Williamson and, surprisingly, the rough and ready Tommy McClennan. Columbia concentrated on Big Bill Broonzy, while Decca put out Blind Boy Fuller material recorded five years earlier.

The Petrillo ban on recording, and a two-year closure of all the studios, led to catalogues being pruned even more heavily. By 1943 Victor had just 75 race records available. It *was* the end of an era, cliché though that may be.

Albert Ammons and Pete Johnson, two of the trio of boogie pianists (Meade Lux Lewis was the other) who defined the fast and frantic style. Johnson also made a series of band sides which influenced the growth of R & B.

Discographers John Godrich and R. M. W. Dixon, who compiled an authoritative 900-page listing of every blues and gospel record made up to 1943, have estimated that 5,500 blues and 1,250 gospel records (many performers recorded both) were issued between 1920 and 1942. Two performers, Tampa Red and Big Bill, each had more than 100 releases; 16 others had 50–100, and 154 more had between 20 and 50. Together, these 172 artists accounted for almost half of all the records issued.

Some recording did go on in the War years. In 1943, for instance, Georgian singer Seth Richards, whose 'Lonely Seth Blues' and 'Skoodeldum Doo' appeared on Columbia in 1928, resurfaced as Skoodle Dum Doo, with an unknown harmonica player called Sheffield, and made four superb country blues and dance sides which could have been reissued from a decade earlier.

But although the older style blues survived and were recorded commercially again in the 1950s (and by field collectors even well into the 1980s), the music was changing and developing.

The recording scene was changing too. Numerous small companies sprang up after the War to meet the demand for black music, and tape recorders were invented, allowing multi-track recording, splicing and the chance for artists to work through a song in the studio before the take to be issued was chosen. John Lee Hooker's various takes of the same song were even sold to different companies under different titles, while Elmore James made numerous attempts at 'Wild About You' before take four was eventually chosen for release.

Even today, as enthusiasts sift through rotting, unlabelled and undocumented tape boxes that survive from the early post-war years, hitherto unsuspected treasures and unknown sessions are still emerging. It seems doubtful, because of the flexibility and reusability of tape, that a completely accurate and comprehensive post-war blues discography will ever be completed, although some labels like Chess have been thoroughly researched and lists are probably as complete as they ever will be.

One of the first post-war labels was Gennett. It had folded in 1934, but owner Harry Gennett had continued working for radio stations, making sound-effects. Joe Davis, a music publisher and singer, made a deal under which he lent Gennett money to refurbish his pressing plant in exchange for Gennett's shellac ration. The new records used old Electrobeam sleeves, but the first issues were 1930 sides by the likes of Big Bill Broonzy and Georgia Tom.

The pre-war Gennett label which Joe Davis revived in the forties.

The Gennett name was soon dropped and renamed Joe Davis. New artists recorded included Gabriel Brown, an excellent Florida singer who had recorded a few tracks for the Library of Congress and was apparently singing in New York streets in the 1950s, despite his sophisticated appearance and unaggressive East Coast style. He made 29 sides for Davis, but sold poorly, and after a few more sides for MGM/Coral reportedly died in a boating accident back in Florida.

Davis also picked up pre-war pianist and former boxer Champion Jack Dupree, who adapted enthusiastically to the new rhythm and blues sound, and who went on to become one of the most recorded bluesmen of all, with hundreds of sides to his credit. He later married and settled in England, and was a popular attraction at European blues festivals.

Davis eventually gave up on blues records, but there were plenty of others to take his place, recording singers on primitive equipment anywhere that took their fancy. There is one hilarious John Lee Hooker record which was made in a shop, and you can hear a customer come in and demand to be served, regardless of John Lee stomping away in front of a mike in the corner.

The small companies were needed because the majors had really lost heart. Victor continued with its old Bluebird favourites, updated slightly with drums and heavier rhythms, while Columbia had Memphis Minnie and Big Bill, but there was a need for new stars who reflected the new age. Victor finally killed the Bluebird label in 1950.

As the First World War had provided new work opportunities for women, so the Second World War gave similar opportunities to blacks. A black middle class was emerging, although as the appalling racism of the 1960s showed, the Deep South resisted any move towards equality for 'uppity Nigras'. And although some black families had more money, the ghettos remained in New York, Detroit and Chicago.

Thousands more blacks headed from the repression in the South to the Northern cities, fuelling the overcrowding and welfare problems. Ironically, they also followed the footsteps of white pioneers, seeking a new life in America's West. Many blues singers followed them, of course, to play in the new black bars in Oakland, which is why so many were recorded in Los Angeles and elsewhere on the West Coast.

Looking back, it is clear that two different musical strands were beginning to emerge: the old-style, downhome blues and a new, jazz-influenced, beat-dominated form, which became known as rhythm and blues (R & B).

R & B was hot. In his notes to a retrospective Atlantic, one of the greatest of all R & B labels, Peter Grendysa defines R & B as 'a loose term encompassing black swing bands, jazz combos, cocktail lounge trios, blues shouters, boogie woogie pianists, down-home guitarists and vocal harmony groups'. Grendysa adds: 'The popularity of this music had increased enormously during the war years and it was beginning to coalesce into a more recognizable type.'

The origins of R & B can be traced back to the swing bands especially the blues-based Kansas City bands like Count Basie (who used blues shouters like Jimmy

Piano Red (aka Dr Feelgood) who recorded with Blind Willie McTell in 1936 and went on to cut some of the wildest post-war boogies (below).

Mr Five by Five, Jimmy Rushing (right), whose blues shouting fronted the Count Basie band for many years.

Lowell Fulson (right), who started as a country blues singer and went on to make hundreds of superb city blues. Still an ace performer today.

Floyd Dixon (below), an immensely popular singer pianist in the more sophisticated nightclub blues style.

Rushing to be heard above the noise of an orchestra at full blast) and Jay McShann.

Another big-voiced shouter was Big Joe Turner. He worked with and recorded regularly with boogie pianist Pete Johnson, and told *down beat* magazine in 1965 how his style developed.

You didn't have microphones or nothing in those days and you got so you could fill one of them big dance halls with one of them little paper horns. And that was something to do then, even if you could get the hang of it – singing to all those hundreds of people.

I used to have a powerful voice before the mikes came in ... but then I found it really made me sing harder. I'd get to singing and it'd sound so good I'd just keep on. I'd get the people all stirred up, just like a preacher.

In fact the Turner-Johnson showcase, 'Roll 'Em Pete', from

Ol' smoothie chops himself.
Charles Brown (above)
whose smarmy vocals and
cocktail piano sold
thousands of records.

Former band leader Jay
McShann (top right), a big
influence on early R & B
who employed top vocalists
– and a young sax player
called Charlie Parker.

A father figure of R & B,
Big Joe Turner (bottom right)
started as a Kansas City
blues shouter with pianist
Pete Johnson and became an
unlikely rock 'n' roll star in
the fifties.

1938, already had many of the trademarks that would be
developed as R & B.

Turner and Johnson had a swinging set of bands
between 1944 and 1954, mainly recording on the West
Coast, before Turner crossed over into the new rock and
roll and had a string of hits, including the original version of 'Shake, Rattle and Roll'. He even recorded with
blues giant Elmore James on one occasion, but most of his
records feature jazz stars taking a break.

Lowell Fulson, who learned his trade with Texas
Alexander and Funny Papa Smith, started his recording
career in a down-home style with his brother Martin on
second guitar. They were charming records, but not what
was wanted, so Fulson soon grew into the new big band
style, with pianists Lloyd Glenn or former bandleader
Jay McShann.

An ultra-smooth style was perfected by Charles
Brown, Floyd Dixon, Nat King Cole, Oscar and Johnny

Moore, and even Ray Charles on his early records. It was gentle, lacking in any real emotion, apart from endless self-pity, and even more swarmy and ingratiating than Lonnie Johnson at his worst. None the less, it seemed to be popular with some record-buyers.

Such blandness was a long way from the work of Texan T-Bone Walker, a veteran from the days of Ma Rainey and the Coley Jones String Band, who pioneered a new, flamboyant guitar technique, using flurries of notes and fast runs on an electric instrument. It was a style that influenced nearly everyone who followed.

Other popular blues shouters included Eddie 'Cleanhead' Vinson, Bull Moose Jackson, Gatemouth Brown, H-Bomb Ferguson, Roy Brown (who wrote 'Good Rocking Tonight', later recorded by Elvis Presley), and the great Wynonie Harris, who combined salaciousness

Ray Charles (left) started as a cocktail blues singer but found fame in a unique blend of blues, jazz and gospel, and, later, country ballads. A major figure on the post-war musical scene.

Who said Jimi Hendrix was original! T-Bone Walker (below left) demonstrates how to play the guitar behind the head (but not why).

Bullmoose Jackson (below right), a singer and sax player from the Lucky Millinder Orchestra.

Eddie 'Cleanhead' Vinson (right), another blues shouter and sax player highly regarded in R & B circles.

Little Willie Littlefield (below right), a superb blues and boogie pianist who made a series of memorable records in the forties and fifties and some less exceptional ones in the eighties.

Clarence 'Gatemouth' Brown (below), a gifted multi-instrumentalist who recorded heavily from the forties onward. He even had a go at the country novelty number 'May the Bird of Paradise Fly Up Your Nose', although his real legacy lies elsewhere!

Wynonie Harris (left), whose
salacious good humour and
raucous vocals were among the
highlights of the R & B era.

Jimmy McCracklin (above), a
prolific West coast R & B
singer and pianist, and a fine
songwriter.

Little Junior Parker (left),
who came out of the
Memphis club scene via Sun
Records and whose hit,
'Mystery Train', was later
recorded by Elvis Presley.
He died in 1971 of a
brain tumour.

Big Maybelle Smith (below),
one of the greatest female
blues shouters. She worked
with the Sweethearts of
Rhythm all-girls band before
the war but adapted enthusiastically to the tougher
sounds of R & B.

and humour with a raucous voice. Roy Brown's crying style influenced B. B. King's vocals, and you can hear it in the early work of Junior Parker, Bobby Bland and even Little Richard, but Brown failed to survive the growth of rock and roll.

Another great name was Louis Jordan, a pre-war swing band leader whose joyful R & B sides like 'Let the Good Times Roll', 'Saturday Night Fish Fry', 'Caldonia' and 'Is You Is or Is You Ain't My Baby' formed the basis for a London show, *Five Guys Named Moe*, some fifty years later.

Among the females were big-voiced women like LaVern Baker, Ruth Brown and Big Maybelle, some of whom successfully crossed over into rock. There were predominantly dance bands, like those of Amos Milburn, Roy Milton, and Joe and Jimmy Liggins, and an amazing touring show, the Johnny Otis Rhythm and Blues Caravan, which featured ballad and blues singers and shouters from Little Esther Phillips and Big Mama

Bobby 'Blue' Bland (left), whose style amalgamated gospel, blues and ballads to make him one of the biggest names in black music.

The Johnny Otis Orchestra of 1962 (below). Otis ran one of the great R & B touring shows and gave a vital break to numerous singers.

Jimmy Wilson (above), a popular fifties singer with a brooding style. His records were often enlivened by the superb West Coast guitarist Lafayette Thomas.

Slide guitarist John Littlejohn (below) made some unissued sides for Chess in 1969 but it took an LP on the Arhoolie label to make his name. An excellent traditional Chicago bluesman.

Louis Jordan (above), whose combination of solid R & B and comedy make him a big seller 50 years after his heyday. There was even a London West End show, *Five Guys Named Moe*, based on his long string of hits.

The highly eccentric, but well named, Screamin' Jay Hawkins (below) whose best records sounded as if he was either stoned or in great pain. Perpetrator of the graphic 'Constipation Blues'.

Percy Mayfield (left), whose sombre blues ballads made him a big star in the fifties.

Roy Brown (above), one of the first soul singers, and writer of numerous hits such as 'Good Rockin' Tonight'. His style of blues shouting influenced a generation of younger singers from Bobby Bland and Little Junior Parker to Little Richard and Jackie Wilson.

Cecil Gant (left), the 'G.I. Sing-sation', who had a lot of hits in the forties with an updated version of the old boogie piano style.

Thornton (a powerful blues singer who first recorded 'Hound Dog', the later Presley hit) to Ivory Joe Hunter and Pee Wee Crayton. Despite pop hits like 'Willie and the Hand Jive', Otis was rooted in the big bands. In the early 1990s he achieved a long-held ambition by recording a whole album of numbers by the likes of Basie and Ellington.

The two R & B singers who achieved the greatest success, both inside and outside the field, were Ray Charles and Fats Domino. Charles began his career singing dreary cocktail blues in the Charles Brown style, but after moving to Atlantic Records, he fused the old gospel call-and-answer style with blues and jazz, going on to produce records of tremendous power and excitement. To hear Charles and the Raelettes roaring out 'The Right Time' (an old Roosevelt Sykes number), 'What'd I Say', or 'Tell the Truth' was an unforgettable, spine-tingling experience. In later years, Charles went on to add country and western to the fusion, with variable

artistic success, although undoubted commercial popularity. Some records still had the Charles magic; his version of 'You Are My Sunshine' or 'I'm Moving On' were as good as any of his earlier R & B screamers.

Fats Domino from New Orleans was a much gentler, more endearing singer, with a piano style rooted in boogie and the loose Kansas City band style. He sang some beautiful blues, although his big hits were more novelty songs, such as 'I'm Going to Be a Wheel Someday' or 'Walking to New Orleans'. But his records sold well outside the R & B world, and Fats is still incredibly popular today. Other New Orleans acts with a big following included Smiley Lewis, Professor Longhair (Henry Roeland Byrd), Huey 'Piano' Smith, and the Neville Brothers.

R & B did not last long in its original forms, gradually taking on elements of country music and forming a new hybrid called rock and roll. Some records marketed as rock were simply R & B with a new name, but the blues element was gradually dissipated. The worst manifestation of the new music was the wheeling out of clean-cut white boys like Pat Boone to make insipid, sometimes censored, covers of black songs, which then vastly outsold the originals.

Wilbert Harrison (above), a singer on the edge of the blues, whose 'Let's Work Together' was a big success for Roxy Music's dapper singer Bryan Ferry.

Johnny Moore and The Three Blazers (below), a slick Nat King Cole style group featuring the sentimental vocals of talented pianist Charles Brown.

Roy Milton (right), one of the real pioneers of R & B, with his band, including Camille Howard, a superlative fast boogie pianist with few equals for speed and inventiveness.

Pianist Joe Liggins (below left) led a very successful R & B band in the fifties, as did his brother guitarist brother, Jimmy.

Little Esther Phillips (below right), one of Johnny Otis' discoveries, who had a big pop hit with 'Release Me'.

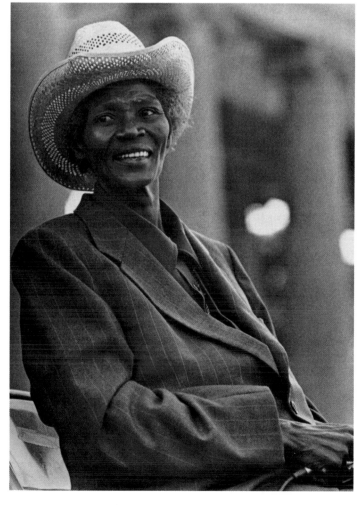

Willie Mae 'Big Mama'
Thornton (left), who made
the original version of 'Hound
Dog' and strongly influenced
white rocker Janis Joplin. One
of the finest female blues
singers of the post-war years.

Pee Wee Crayton (above),
a West Coast singer and
guitarist, who made some
good sides for Modern and
Imperial in the forties and
fifties.

That criticism hardly applies to Elvis Presley, of course. He was steeped in the blues and used the blues songs he recorded with respect, not copying the originals but adding something of his own to make a hybrid which was fresh and original. Presley's Sun recordings, his first, are superb examples of early fusion music and have an undeniable authenticity and authority which are not affected by his later excesses.

Alongside R & B the old blues still flourished and was still being recorded. Hundreds of tiny record companies appeared, some of which issued only a few singles before vanishing. Others, like Atlantic, Chess and Specialty, were bigger operations that still exist today in one form or another.

There were the entrepreneurs, too: Bob Geddins with the influential West Coast Down Town, Big Town and Rhythm Labels, Sam Phillips in Memphis with Sun,

Johnny 'Guitar' Watson (left), a powerful West Coast performer who made some fine blues sides before turning to disco music.

The big wheel himself. Fats Domino (below left), whose attractive brand of New Orleans music took him out of R & B and into the lucrative rock 'n' roll market where he had numerous big hits.

New Orleans R & B singer Smiley Lewis (below right) never found the success of Fats Domino, but made the original version of the Presley hit, 'One Night'. Elvis had to censor the words slightly to get the record played on air.

Professor Longhair, whose 'Mardi Gras in New Orleans' from 1949 is still the carnival theme. His real name was Henry Roeland (Roy) Byrd and his bands included the Shuffling Hungarians and the Blues Scholars.

Don Robey with Peacock and Duke, the Bihari brothers with Modern and RPM, Bill Quinn and Gold Star, Art Rupe with Specialty, Fred Mendelssohn with Regal and Bob Shad of Sittin' In With were just some. Other important blues labels included JOB, Aristocrat (the predecessor of Chess), Apollo, Cobra, Parrot, Excello, Aladdin and Vee-Jay.

Yet in the beginning there were few independent studios, and many of the independents had to rely on the majors for studio space, mastering and pressing. The main recording centres were therefore where the studios were – Los Angeles and San Francisco in the West, Chicago and Detroit in the North; New Orleans, Lake Charles, Crowley and Jackson in the Deep South; Memphis and Nashville in Tennessee; New York and Philadelphia in the East; Houston, Dallas and San Antonio in Texas. Many recordings, however, were still made on portable equipment or at radio stations.

Gold Star, one small company better documented than most, thanks to Chris Strachwitz who has leased the masters for his Arhoolie label, was a typical hap-

hazard operation. It was started by Bill Quinn, a radio repairer in Houston, Texas, who began recording messages for people to send to friends and relatives. In his notes to a Gold Star reissue CD, Strachwitz wrote:

During the war, Bill Quinn and his partner set up a single press and learned how to make not only the acetate recordings, but also how to process them and form the metal masters. Due to the shellac shortage, they had difficulty getting material for their records and would hold 'biscuit days' from time to time, when the public was asked to bring in their old records and were paid 10 cents each so they could be melted down and used for new pressings.

Quinn had a hard time not only learning how to press records but how to process his master acetates and prepare the stampers. There was no book to learn them from and the big companies apparently refused to share their secrets.

Gold Star was started in 1946 and the first release was by Cajun fiddler Harry Choates. It was so successful that the big Modern company in Los Angeles licensed it for national distribution. Unfortunately, Bill Quinn knew nothing about copyright, so when the song, the Cajun anthem 'Jole Blon,' was covered by big names like Roy Acuff, he and Choates got nothing from it.

The First Gold Star blues release was 'Short Haired Woman' and 'Big Mama Jump' by one of the best blues singers of all time, Lightnin' Hopkins. It became a regional hit.

Lightnin' was a true folk poet, a man who could make up a song on the spot when he needed cash, and whose music ranged from moody, deeply emotional blues to jaunty dance tunes. The long series of records he made for Gold Star and other labels like Aladdin and Modern, which bought Quinn masters, are undoubtedly his best, although he went on to record powerful rhythm and blues with a small band and hundreds of sides for other companies.

His skill at improvisation was breathtaking, as were the variations he achieved on a comparatively small number of themes. Hopkins recorded for anyone who would pay him, but interest in his music waned around 1954. It took white enthusiasts like Sam Charters and Mack McCormick to launch him on a new career as a college, concert and club performer. Many of his later records were routine and a bit complacent, but his Gold Stars will remain his greatest legacy. He died in 1982,

Lightnin' Hopkins (left), the premier blues poet on a flyer for the Gold Star label for which he made a series of musical masterpieces.

Eddie 'Guitar Slim' Jones (above), slightly eccentric but influential New Orleans musician, best known for the classic 'The Things I Used to Do'. He died at the age of 33.

but at least his European fans had a chance to see him on tour.

After Hopkins, Quinn's best seller was Lil' Son Jackson, a fan of Lemon Jefferson, who had sent Gold Star a test record he made in an amusement arcade. He was very different to Hopkins, with a hypnotic, loping guitar and light, plaintive voice that was instantly attractive. He recorded 10 sides, plus a couple for Modern, before being picked up by Imperial for a long series of excellent R & B sides. There were more recordings in the Gold Star style for Arhoolie before he died in the mid-1970s.

Quinn also recorded some lesser-known artists, such as drummer L. C. Williams, a friend and disciple of Lightnin'; Wilson 'Thunder' Smith, who accompanied Lightnin' on his first record for Aladdin in 1946 (the one at which the elderly Texas Alexander was due to record); and others like Buddy Chiles, Andy Thomas, Perry Cain and Isam Hisam, who may have been friends of Lightnin' but are otherwise unknown.

Not everything Quinn recorded was issued; collectors would love to hear the sides by down-home singer Wright Holmes, which Quinn rejected as too similar to Lightnin'. Other performances were simply lost when the manufacturing process went wrong (there were no copies made of the original acetates). Only 100 copies were made of the rarest Hopkins coupling, 'Jazz Blues' and 'Henny Penny Blues', because a bad hum developed somewhere along the line.

But there was plenty of demand to record from blues hopefuls. Quinn offered facilities to other companies who came to Houston with portable recorders, including the Shads of Sittin' In With. They had advertised for potential artists just as Victor used to do on its field trips in the 1920s. The result was a long queue of black men just waiting for a chance, and who knows what major talents were missed.

The Gold Star label lasted just five years – killed in the end by the loss of Lightnin' to bigger companies, the death of Harry Choates and massive tax liabilites. Numerous other little companies could have told similar stories, but somehow a large number of traditional, Southern-style blues did get recorded and, somehow, most of them have survived as battered acetates, tapes or 78s.

Memphis was a major centre for blues recording and much of the local talent was herded towards the Bihari brothers' Modern, RPM, Meteor and Flair labels by Ike Turner, a pianist and band leader, later to find much greater fame with his wife, Tina.

Many of the blues sides were recorded by Sam Phillips, a white disc jockey from Alabama, who opened his own studio, Memphis Recording Service, in 1950, and either leased sides to Chess and the Biharis, or put them out on his own Phillips and Sun labels. Until 1954, he cut most of his records directly on to acetates, but it was the extra flexibility of tape which allowed him to create the famous Sun sound – a tape delay echo heard to great effect on early Presley sides. But tape was expensive and he had to re-use reels over and over again. Hours of out-takes, rejected masters and alternate versions, including much of Presley's early work, were simply recorded over.

Phillips liked down-home blues, and recorded old-timers Charlie Burse from the Memphis Jug Band, Jack Kelly from the South Memphis Jug Band (only a fragment survives) and Sleepy John Estes. But there were other, newer acts to whom he gave a chance, including Joe Hill Louis, a talented and rather jolly one-man band,

and a young singer-guitarist with great promise called B. B. King. He placed both with the Biharis.

Then there was Jackie Brenston, who played with Ike Turner's Kings of Rhythm, singing a storming boogie called 'Rocket 88', which Phillips sold to Chess. It became a huge hit and Phillips always claimed it was the first real rock and roll record. The Biharis, however, were upset he hadn't offered it to them, so the Modern/RPM group decided to go it alone in Memphis. Ike Turner joined them as talent scout and found them numerous rural acts of considerable quality, including Houston Boines, Elmore James copyist Boyd Gilmore (part of an Elmore record was even spliced on to one of

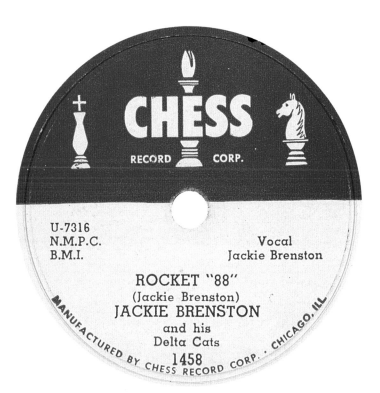

Howlin' Wolf (left), one of
the most awesome performers
of the blues. A huge man
with a mighty voice, his
electrified Mississippi blues
have an unequalled power
and ferocity.

Blues on tour (right).
Backstage with (from left)
Lafayette Leake, Willie
Dixon, Buster Benton, Jimmy
Dawkins, and Big Walter
Horton.

Rosco Gordon (left), one of
the Memphis R & B giants,
over whom the Chess and
Bihari brothers fought. The
Biharis got Gordon, Chess
got Howling Wolf instead.

Harmonica player Sammy
Lewis (above), whose 1955
duets with guitarist Willie
Johnson were among the best
sides ever issued by Sam
Phillips on his Sun label.

his sides) and the Drifting Slim Band with Baby Face
Turner, Junior Brooks and Sunny Blair. But it was
Phillips who first recorded the man he regarded as the
best of the lot: Howlin' Wolf.

Wolf (real name Chester Burnett) was a massive man
with a voice to match. He'd been brought up in
Mississippi and enjoyed the music of Charley Patton;
indeed, his voice echoed the dark coarseness of Patton
with added volume. Phillips recalled, 'When I heard
him, I said, "This is for me. This where the soul of man
never dies."'

Phillips first recorded Wolf in 1951 and sent dubs to
both the Biharis and the Chess brothers. They both
wanted Wolf, and for a time he would record for
Phillips in Memphis then nip across to West Memphis
to do some of the same songs for RPM. In the end, Wolf
went to Chess, and the Biharis kept Rosco Gordon over
whom the two companies were also squabbling.

Wolf moved to Chicago and one of his first releases
there was a Memphis recording, 'Just My Kind', a version of 'Roll and Tumble', which was terrifying in its
speed, volume and ferocity. Wolf became one of the sta-
ple acts of Chess in Chicago, and even had a Top 30 pop
hit with 'Smokestack Lightnin'', a record that owed a
lot to Patton and Tommy Johnson.

Those who saw Wolf on tour in Britain still speak in
awe of the amazing power this giant figure generated on
stage. He even, reluctantly, made a 1960s psychedelic
album which he summed up pithily as 'dogshit'.

Sam Phillips's obituary for him when he died in 1976 described him perfectly. 'He had no voice in the sense of a pretty voice, but he had command of every word he spoke. When the beat got going in the studio, he would sit there and sing, hypnotizing himself. Wolf was one of those raw people. Dedicated. Natural.'

Other blues acts recorded by Phillips included Walter Horton, a veteran harmonica player, whose instrumental 'Easy' is perhaps the finest of its kind ever recorded; disc jockey Rufus Thomas who made 'Bear Cat', Sun's first national hit and a thinly disguised rewrite of 'Hound Dog'; Little Junior Parker, a slick R & B singer whose records included 'Mystery Train', which Presley recorded two years later; Little Milton Campbell, whose Sun style was described by label historian Colin Escott as 'a paint by numbers approach to the blues'; James Cotton and Pat Hare, whose heavily distorted 'Cotton Crop Blues' is a genuine post-war classic; and another one-man band and very fine singer, Dr Ross.

Then Phillips recorded a young white kid called Elvis Presley, who sang the blues like the blacks, and the course of music history changed.

He wears short shorts! Rufus Thomas (above) demonstrates the lighter side of the blues!

Elmore James (right), whose 'Dust My Broom' riff electrified British blues bands. He was described by one of the few white collectors who saw him as the most exciting performer of the lot.

Walter Horton and Floyd Jones (left), two of the stalwarts of Chicago blues. Horton, a veteran of the Memphis Jug Band era, made one of the all time great instrumental blues, 'Easy', for Sun records before moving to Chicago. Floyd Jones' Tommy Johnson-inspired blues from the fifties are now collectors items.

Dr Isaiah Ross (below), a superb one man band, who recorded dozens of sides for Sun in the fifties which are only now being issued. A highly gifted performer.

Another down-South label of some importance was Trumpet in Jackson, Mississippi, which was run by Lillian McMurry. She made the first recordings by the second Sonny Boy Williamson (Aleck Rice Miller), another post-war giant, whose sides for Trumpet with a small band epitomize the sound of Mississippi in the 1950s. They might not have the tight coherence of Sonny Boy's later Chess sides, but they feature many of his trademarks: uncanny timing, quavering voice, finger-snapping and short, stabbing harmonica phrases. Among them were the influential 'Nine Below Zero' and 'Eyesight to the Blind', which Eric Clapton performed in The Who's rock opera film, *Tommy* (1975). Some of these early sides were not issued until the late 1980s.

Sonny Boy was another who went on to become a mainstay of the Chess label in Chicago, recording many fine city blues with a heavy country overlay. He toured Britain and Europe in the 1960s, delighting audiences with his city gent's bowler hat and suit in two shades of grey (divided vertically). He died in 1965 in Helena, Arkansas, where efforts are being made to set up a museum in his honour.

Trumpet also recorded the ubiquitous Big Joe Williams, who produced some of his fastest and grittiest solo sides; Willie Love, a warm-voiced singer-pianist with a tight little band; Mississippi's Arthur 'Big Boy' Crudup, whose Victor contract had expired, so he made two sides for cash in hand; Luther and Percy Huff, a mandolin and guitar duo producing a glorious, anachronistic country sound that could have been recorded in the 1920s (they'd played with Patton, Tommy Johnson and Ishmon Bracey, among others). Last, but not least, Trumpet recorded Elmore James.

James, who had been singing around Mississippi for years, had a hard, intense, agonized voice that would carry across noisy clubs. He was the definitive electric bluesman, using his guitar and amp to create sounds not possible on an acoustic instrument. Among the people he had played with was Robert Johnson, from whom he had picked up a walking bass figure and 'Dust My Broom', which became his best-known song. James, however, transformed Johnson's slide style into a frantic, electrified riffing that grabbed the attention immediately. The record was issued with unknown Bobo Thomas singing the old Delta standard 'Catfish Blues' under James's name. Prior to this he had been working with Willie Love (he recorded in his band for Trumpet) and helped out on some Sonny Boy Williamson sessions.

Homesick James Williamson (above), cousin of Elmore James, who carried on the electric slide tradition.

Hound Dog Taylor (below), one of the best Elmore James disciples and an effective electric slide guitarist. He made a few unissued records for Chess but his career was really launched by Bruce Iglauer's Alligator label in the seventies.

The King Bee. Slim Harpo (James Moore), whose laid back delivery and warm voice made him one of the best of the Louisiana swamp bluesmen (right). He died of a heart attack before he could benefit from his popularity in Europe.

The following year James started a long series of recordings for the Biharis. These produced some of his rawest and most dramatic sides, including 'I Believe', 'Please Find My Baby' and 'Hand in Hand'. There were plenty of 'Dust My Broom' variations, but he used shuffle rhythms, country boogies and unbearably introvert, slow blues as well.

Although he faced serious health problems, he weathered competition from the new sound of rock and roll, and remained popular in Chicago. He recorded for the new Chief label with Jimmy Reed sidekick Eddie Taylor, for Chess and for the New York Fire label, where some of his best-known songs, like 'The Sky Is Crying' and 'It Hurts Me Too', were cut. Union problems halted his career in Chicago for a while, but he re-

corded steadily, including one last (stereo) session in 1963, before a heart attack killed him.

Few white blues enthusiasts ever saw James, or had even heard of him at the time. One who did, the Belgian Georges Adins, called him 'the most exciting and dramatic blues singer that I've ever heard'. His sound lived on in the work of his cousin, Homesick James Williamson, Chicago club singer J. B. Hutto, and Hound Dog Taylor among bluesmen, and in the rock music of Brian Jones, Jeff Beck, Duane Allman and, in particular, Jeremy Spencer of the early Fleetwood Mac.

Apart from the R & B scene in New Orleans, which produced offbeat characters such as Professor Longhair and his Spanish-tinged Mardi Gras music, old forms of blues were still being recorded by labels like Goldband, Khoury, Jin and Excello elsewhere in Louisiana.

Excello specialized in what became known as swamp blues – lazy, Jimmy Reed-style vocals, relaxed Caribbean-influenced backings, echoey guitar and mouth organ – what one poetically inclined sleeve-note writer described as 'a cricket-chirpin', frog-croakin', Spanish Moss-drippin' sound'. Most of the best swamp blues were recorded by J. D. Miller at Crowley and passed on to Excello in Nashville. His best artists included Lightnin' Slim, a superb, rough, country bluesman, Slim Harpo,

J B Hutto (above), a disciple of Elmore James with a violent, rough sound that never fails to excite. His magnificent 1954 records for Chance are among the best Chicago blues of the fifties.

Lightnin' Slim (Otis Hicks), greatest of the Louisiana swamp bluesmen (right). One of the finest down-home artists to record since the war, his blues-drenched voice and lazy guitar sum up everything that is meant by swamp blues. Moses 'Whispering' Smith, another Louisiana stalwart, here plays the harmonica.

wistful and more sophisticated, Lonesome Sundown and Lazy Lester. Another Excello singer, Arthur Gunter, had a minor hit with 'Baby Let's Play House' – another blues better known through a Presley recording.

Numerous other old-style singers were recorded by other companies. Regal records picked up Blind Willie McTell and Curley Weaver yet again for their best post-war sides, plus a superb slide guitarist called Dennis McMillan from North Carolina, pre-war Georgia harmonica player Frank Edwards, and a few more minor figures like Pee Wee Hughes and David Wylie.

Gotham in Philadelphia had one superlative session by Dan Pickett, an experienced musician with an East Coast flavour, whose music hinted at a familiarity with that of Blind Boy Fuller and Tampa Red. That was the beginning and end of his recording career – a few extremely high-quality blues and boogies with ringing bottleneck, and then Pickett (real name James Founty, and a man of major talent) vanished forever. Most of the sides weren't even issued until the 1980s.

Gotham also had Doug Quattlebaum, a heavy-voiced singer from South Carolina, one of whose records has been issued unedited to great effect on CD; Ralph Willis, a Blind Boy Fuller disciple from Alabama; Texan Wright Holmes, a wild and eccentric singer-guitarist; the lugubrious Stickhorse Hammond; and even Muddy Waters' first commercial record – a rather dull version of 'Mean Red Spider', issued in 1946 as by James Carter.

Recordings such as these, however were really looking back. The future was being made in cities like Chicago, New York and Detroit.

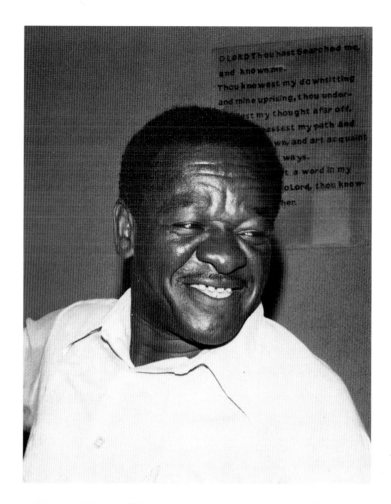

Between 1940 and 1960 more than 3 million black people left the Southern states and headed for cities like Chicago, Detroit, New York and Los Angeles. Northern businessmen actively encouraged it, especially during the war when labour from Europe became unavailable, and by 1960, three-quarters of all blacks in the USA were living in cities or big towns.

Chicago was a favourite destination for blacks from the rich blues areas of Mississippi, Arkansas, Louisiana and Tennessee, thanks to the Illinois Central railroad which ran from New Orleans for nearly 1,000 miles to Chicago. Between 1940 and 1950 alone 154,000 blacks moved to Chicago, by far the greatest number coming from Mississippi. The city had long been a centre for the blues, with Memphis Minnie, Sonny Boy Williamson and

Red Rooster Bar, a typical
small Harlem bar (right).

Lonesome Sundown (Cornelius
Green), another of the J D
Miller stable of Louisiana
swamp blues performers
(opposite, above).

Lazy Lester (real name
Leslie Johnson), one of the
big four of the swamp blues
sound recorded in the J D
Miller studios in Louisiana
(opposite, below).

The Apollo Theatre, New
York (below).

Big Bill playing the numerous clubs that studded the main Negro area on the south side. There was also a big open-air market on Maxwell Street, where singers newly in from the South played for the crowds and sought that elusive first break. Victor and Columbia were still recording the veterans as the 1940s drew to a close, but it was left to the independents to chronicle the new city blues that was developing.

The first independent label was probably Rhumboogie in 1945, which managed three releases by the slick T-Bone Walker before disappearing. R & B singer Jo Jo Adams appeared on a Melody Lane and Hy Tone label, but these and other minor companies concentrated on the jump blues and ballads. It was left to the tiny Ora Nelle label to make the first historic recordings of the newly updated country style.

Ora Nelle was founded in 1947 by Bernard Abrams of the Maxwell Radio Record Company, and issued only two singles. (Its acetates survived, however, and were finally issued by a small American label nearly 40 years later.) The first single featured a young harmonica player, influenced like most by Sonny Boy Williamson. He called himself Little Walter and recorded with Mississippi guitarist Othum Brown whose song, 'Ora Nelle Blues', may have given the label its curious name. It was a lovely down-home sound but probably didn't make much money.

The other single was by guitarist Johnny Williams, who had learned his trade in the Delta, and fast-fingered mandolinist Johnny Young, who had picked up his style from the Mississippi Sheiks. This is another record prized by collectors which didn't sell at the time, and Ora Nelle quietly disappeared. But it also recorded old-timers Sleepy John Estes (on a truly moving blues about the effects of blindness), Johnny Temple, and Willie McNeal, a young guitarist calling himself Boll Weevil.

Another early independent was Planet, which picked up another Sonny Boy disciple, Snooky Pryor, and guitarist Moody Jones, a highly talented musician who was at home in all kinds of music, from Irish to hillbilly; he was even photographed in a cowboy outfit. Planet also recorded Moody's cousin, Floyd, who became a mainstay of the Chicago scene and recorded for JOB, Chess and Vee-Jay. Other small companies of short life and tiny output included Tempo Tone, Marvel, Old Swingmaster and Miracle, some of whose recordings are both rare and much sought after by enthusiasts. The most important label, however, was undoubtedly Chess, which started life in 1947 as Aristocrat.

The Chess brothers Leonard and Phil, were Polish immigrants who ran bars and a club featuring black popular singers such as Ella Fitzgerald and Billy Eckstine. They set up Aristocrat to record jump blues and jazz, the precursors of R & B, but in 1947 pianist

Sunnyland Slim, who had previously made records for Victor imitating the eccentric, irritating and deceased Dr Clayton, talked them into a recording session. With him he brought a friend and colleague, guitarist Muddy Waters.

Waters' first recordings by the Library of Congress in Mississippi in 1941 and 1942 had been beautiful examples of the rich Delta tradition handed down particularly by Son House. Waters moved to Chicago in 1943, working in a factory and playing for house parties and eventually in the clubs, with friendly encouragement from Big Bill and Sonny Boy Williamson. He first recorded commercially in 1946, a dull 1930s-style number called 'Mean Red Spider', which he reworked far more effectively for Chess two years later. There was also another, unissued, session for Lester Melrose and Columbia, which sounded like every other Melrose act. Surprisingly, the normally canny Melrose was beginning to lose his touch and failed to spot his potential.

Waters worked with guitarist Jimmy Rogers, later to be a vital member of his band, pianists Eddie Boyd and Sunnyland Slim, jazz-influenced guitarist Blue Smitty (Claude Smith) and the affable guitarist and drummer Baby Face Leroy Foster. His first four sides for Chess were frankly ordinary, but Leonard Chess, with some bewilderment, overheard him playing in the bottleneck style he had recorded in 1941.

Snooky Pryor (above), one of the bedrocks of Chicago blues, whose early recordings as leader, and in support of, Floyd Jones and others, are much prized classics.

Sunnyland Slim (below), a raucous singer and pianist and a mainstay of the Chicago scene for more than half a century.

Site of Maxwell Radio Record Company, Maxwell Street, Chicago (left). This was once home to Ora Nelle Records for whom Little Walter first recorded.

Theresa's lounge on Chicago's South Side (below), home to many artists such as Junior Wells and James Cotton.

His next single coupled reworkings of two of those LOC sides with just a bass player (and added electricity). They were magnificent, one a jaunty dance tune and the other a dark sombre blues, but both with the raw Delta bottleneck sound. Chicago record-buyers loved them, and until 1950, Waters recorded a number of what were little more than electrified versions of Mississippi blues from a generation before.

At the same time he was working with a band in the clubs, but Chess didn't want that kind of sound. So in 1950 Waters, Little Walter (by now a vital part of the Muddy Waters sound) and Baby Face Leroy did a moonlighting session for the new Parkway label. The results were superb, but a two-part version of the old Delta standard, 'Rollin' and Tumblin'', was for many collectors the finest recorded Chicago blues of all. It was a truly extraordinary record, with humming and moaning, a frantic vocal and Waters' bottleneck fighting with Little Walter's harmonica in an atmosphere of mounting tension. Chess were furious and a chastened Waters had

Eddie Boyd (above), a widely recorded Chicago singer-pianist who wrote many memorable songs including 'Five Long Years'. He toured Europe extensively and settled in Paris and Helsinki.

Muddy Waters (right), unchallenged king of the Chicago blues, whose hundreds of records are an unrivalled legacy. To the right is Waters' pianist, Otis Spann, whose own recordings from the fifties and sixties are generally much sought after.

to make another version of 'Rollin' and Tumblin'' which was a pale shadow of the original.

It was around this time, too, that Waters and Little Walter duetted on an exquisite record called 'Louisiana Blues', which has an enduring beauty and wistful quality, underscored by a gently melodic guitar and harmonica working in perfect harmony.

Waters was soon to leave the delta bottleneck style behind, although it resurfaced occasionally to stunning effect on some later sides. His style became tougher, more city orientated than his early country sides. Musicians included harmonica players Junior Wells, Walter Horton and James Cotton, pianists Otis Spann and Henry Gray, and the powerful bass player and entrepreneur Willie Dixon, whose songs and arrangements dominated Chicago blues for a decade.

At each stage of his development, Waters' records represented the very best of that style, and his 200 or so Chess sides to 1967 are a remarkable document of the way Chicago blues grew up.

Waters toured England several times. On the first occasion, in 1958, he petrified audiences used to the gentler sound of Big Bill and Lonnie Johnson with his huge, amplified electric sound. Few people then realized that this was the current sound of the blues in the Chicago clubs, not a recreation of a dead era.

In 1967 Waters left Chess and started a new career under the guidance of white guitarist Johnny Winter. He died in 1983, leaving a wealth of recordings, including one last session, issued on a bootleg LP, with the Rolling Stones, who took their name from one of his earliest and most memorable records.

Little Walter, a tough and quarrelsome character, went his own way, and had big hits with a lively instrumental, 'Juke', and 'My Babe', a Willie Dixon rewrite of the old gospel song, 'This Train'. He had a quiet, sad voice but his amplified harmonica was imaginative and disciplined, unlike his life. He died in 1968 from injuries suffered in a street fight.

Little Walter Jacobs (left) who revolutionised amplified harmonica playing and was one of the founding fathers of the post-war Chicago sound.

The godfather of the blues, Willie Dixon (top left) who dominated Chicago blues for 30 years.

Jimmy Rogers, who played and toured with Muddy Waters from 1950 to 1956, also made his own records. 'That's Alright', in a more relaxed and polished style than Waters, was a good seller, but he was equally influential in helping to forge the early Chicago style. Otis Spann, a breathy singer but fine pianist, had an extensive career outside the Waters band until his death from cancer in 1970. James Cotton is still playing and recording at the time of writing, although to some extent living in the shadow of his work for Sun and with Waters.

The other Chess giants were Howlin' Wolf and Sonny Boy Williamson No. 2, who had, like Waters moved up from the South. There was also J. B. Lenoir, a very different artist with a high-pitched voice and swinging guitar style, and un unusual sense of political correctness. He recorded blues about the Korean War and President Eisenhower, and ran into problems with the censor; a 1960s' album for CBS attacked segregation and the Vietnam War so pungently that the album was never released in the USA.

Some of Chess's signings never really made it big outside their own communities, and sometimes not even there. Big Boy Spires, John Brim, Honeyboy Edwards, Rocky Fuller (Louisiana Red), Little Johnnie Jones and

many others made records for Chess (or for companies that sold masters to Chess), but rarely gained commercial success. Some did, such as Willie Mabon, a likeable piano entertainer, Lowell Fulson, the Oklahoma R & B singer who first made his name on the West Coast, and Koko Taylor, a hard-voiced woman who had a big hit

James Cotton (above), a veteran from the early days of Sun in Memphis, and from one of Muddy Waters best bands. Still a fine harmonica player but a rather poor singer.

J B Lenoir's courageous, political blues about President Eisenhower and the Korean War got him into trouble with the authorities. An unusual, high-voiced singer (left), he made many excellent sides for Parrot, Chess and JOB in the fifties.

John Brim (above), who, with wife Grace, made some of the best of the early post-war Chicago blues records.

Willie Mabon (below), who made a series of sophisticated and humorous blues in the fifties and sixties.

Jimmy Rogers (above), one of the founders of modern Chicago blues and an important member of the early Muddy Waters bands. His own hits included 'That's All Right' and 'Ludella'.

Koko Taylor (below), a tough vocalist on the edge of R & B and rock and one of the few women blues singers still performing in Chicago.

with 'Wang Wang Doodle' and is still performing in Chicago today.

While Chess picked up most of the potential sellers, other record labels, like JOB, Cobra and Parrot, gave many aspiring singers a chance.

JOB was run by Joe Brown and singer St Louis Jimmy Oden, and it was something of a ramshackle operation. The first record was a very old-fashioned side by the obscure Stick Horse Hammond, which not even Joe Brown remembered in later years. JOB also recorded Snooky Pryor, Sunnyland Slim, Eddie Boyd, J. B. Lenoir, the magnificent Delta bluesman and Robert Johnson associate Johnny Shines, Robert Junior Lockwood (Johnson's stepson), John and Grace Brim, and Floyd Jones. Many originally unissued sides have since been released in England by the enthusiasts' label Flyright.

Chance Records started in 1950 and their small output includes some sides of high quality by Sunnyland Slim, bottleneck guitarist Homesick James, piano-pounder Lazy Bill Lucas, and (best of all) the thunderous, declamatory Elmore James imitator, J. B. Hutto.

United and States Records had Robert Nighthawk, who sang Tommy Johnson's 'Maggie Campbell' for them,

and Junior Wells, another Sonny Boy disciple whose earliest sides are brilliant, inventive blues that rivalled Little Walter for skill and technique. There were also a couple of sides by Memphis harmonica player Walter 'Shakey' Horton, who never really repeated the innovatory sound of his Sun sides.

Parrot and Blue Lake had some superb releases, including Sunnyland Slim's *tour de force*, 'Going Back to Memphis' ('Rolling and Tumbling' yet again, but with pounding piano and dynamic vocal), and Little Willie Foster's exciting 'Falling Rain Blues'.

Another major source of quality blues was Vee Jay, started by Vivian Carter and Jimmy Bracken in 1953. Their roster included Floyd Jones, Eddie Taylor, Big Joe Williams (now heavily amplified) and Billy Boy Arnold, a new singer of fairly average ability. Their big star, however, was Jimmy Reed, a lazy, nasal singer almost totally devoid of emotion, but whose records, including 'Baby What You Want Me to Do', 'Hush Hush' and 'Bright Lights Big City', sold well and were widely copied by Louisiana singers such as Slim Harpo and Jimmy Anderson, and British imitators. Sadly, Reed overshadowed his partner, Eddie Taylor, a much better

Sammy Myers (opposite, top) played with Elmore James and recorded a handful of singles in the fifties and sixties. His more recent albums

Louis Myers of The Three Aces (opposite, bottom), the band which Little Walter took over from Junior Wells and renamed The Jukes. His musician parents had played with Charley Patton and Blind Boy Fuller.

Fifties Chicago house (left) party with, from left, Mac Thompson, Billy Boy Arnold, Reynolds Howard (back), a fan called Milton (front) and the influential but little known Jody Williams.

His singing was desultory, his instrumental technique basic, but Jimmy Reed's lazy style (above) was very popular and influential.

Eddie Taylor (below), a fine Chicago bluesman, who remained in the shadow of the less talented (but more popular) Jimmy Reed. His own 'Big Town Playboy' was an influential hit.

all-round bluesman, who had some success with 'Big Town Playboy'.

There were other companies based in Chicago's west side, the other main black area, the most important of which was Cobra. Their big discovery was Otis Rush, a young singer with a very dramatic style influenced by B. B. King's way of singing gospel-style against a guitar played with fast, single-note runs more common to jazz. King had become very popular with a string of hits on the West Coast for RPM, and was to go on to international stardom, but at this point he was a model for the next generation of players.

Otis Rush sang in a tortured, crying style, full of emotion and intensity and backed by a sax-led R & B band. Some of his ballad sides, such as 'Violent Love', were unbelievably dire, but at his best on 'Double Trouble', 'I Can't Quit You Baby', or 'Groaning the Blues' he was magnificent. Rush also recorded for Chess, to lesser effect, and is still active today.

Cobra also had Magic Sam Maghett, a brilliant guitarist but limited singer whose records lacked variety. However, the finest of all Cobra's artists was undoubtedly Buddy Guy from Louisiana. Guy had recorded ineffec-

tually in Baton Rouge, but moved to Chicago in the mid-1950s, where he met Rush and Magic Sam, who introduced him to Cobra. If Rush was unrestrained, Guy verged on the hysterical, with something akin to imminent breakdown found in Robert Johnson's wilder numbers. His Cobra sides are good, but nowhere near as powerful as his large output for Chess from 1960 where his screaming vocals and wailing guitar had an energy and violence few others have achieved.

Guy was held back by Chess when he wanted to join the rock revolution. Later, in 1968, Leonard Chess begged Guy to kick him for not allowing him to record the kind of electric blues that were selling millions for Jimi Hendrix and Cream. Guys records, however, are masterly, ranging from the slow, moody blues of 'My Time After Awhile', the histrionics of 'First Time I Met the Blues', the jazz of Art Blakey's theme tune, 'Moaning', and even the girly group soul of 'Lip Lap Louie'. The CD reissue of his complete Chess recordings includes unedited takes, which show how he could really build up tension and interest over a long period.

Another Chicago label was Chief, which recorded Elmore James, Junior Wells, Magic Sam and slide gui-

His real name was Sam Maghett (left), but he was Magic Sam on record. He made some fine sides but died before he could develop his full potential.

Three of the best of the post-war Chicago scene (right). Pianist Eddie Boyd [left], flamboyant singer-guitarist Buddy Guy and drummer Fred Below [right].

Otis Rush (opposite left), whose anguished early recordings for Cobra and Chess rank among the best to come from West Side Chicago.

Artistic

Armel Music
BMI 2:35
C 1060

Vocal
1503

YOU SURE CAN'T DO
(L. P. Weaver)
Buddy Guy
and his Band

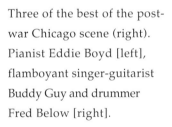

Earl Hooker (left), who rarely sang but played solid slide guitar on many small labels. Collectors prize his early sides with Pinetop Perkins, Junior Wells, and his later albums for Chris Strachwitz's ground-breaking Arhoolie label.

Texas one-man band Weldon 'Juke Boy' Bonner (below) got his nickname for being a human jukebox, willing to play anything he was asked. But despite extensive recording and strong support from the British magazine *Blues Unlimited*, he failed to make it big and drank himself to death.

tarist Earl Hooker, while the Bea and Baby label, run by a character called Cadillac Baby, put out some collectable sides by Homesick James, James Cotton, Hound Dog Taylor, Sunnyland Slim and Little Mac Simmons, among others.

Only one new label, USA, appeared in the 1960s. It featured J. B. Lenoir, Willie Mabon and T. V. Slim, plus Homesick James playing Robert Johnson's 'Crossroads'. It seemed as if the blues had come full circle.

But not all blues music was to be found in Chicago. There was a busy scene in Detroit, too, based on the clubs and bars of Hastings Street. Singers who had travelled up from the South included Calvin Frazier, who had recorded for the Library of Congress, Baby Boy Warren from Memphis, Bo Bo Jenkins from Arkansas, Eddie Burns from Mississippi, and Eddie Kirkland from Louisiana. The car factories drew them to what would later be nicknamed Motown.

Big Maceo performer here, as did Dr Ross, while Joe Von Battle recorded anyone vaguely promising, even One String Sam, a primitive street singer whose one-string instrument sounded like something from the remote reaches of Africa. Record companies included JVB, Fortune, Big Star and King from Cincinnati, but one artist dominated Detroit above all others. He was John Lee Hooker.

Hooker came up from Mississippi, but his style was unique – at least, no one has ever traced its antecedants.

Eddie 'Guitar' Burns (above), best known for his partnership with John Lee Hooker, but an effective bluesman in his own right.

Mandolin player Johnny Young (below) was right in there at the beginning of post-war Chicago blues but never made it big himself.

He played with a heavy boogie beat, although not the style of boogie associated with the piano. His style involved deliberately erratic timing and fragmented chords, often with a chilling sense of menace or doom. Hooker enthusiast Dave Sax notes on a Krazy Kat record sleeve:

> Many of the chords that John locates on his guitar do not seem to be in any book, a fact that perplexes would-be imitators. Other times he picks out complex sequences of individual notes, or sings in unison to spartan clusters played on the bass strings. On still other occasions, bent, undocumented chords, aided by loud amplification, become hypnotic drones.

Hooker was working in a factory and playing by night when he was noticed by record store owner Elmer Barbee. Some of the earliest audition records Hooker made for Barbee in 1948 still exist and were finally issued by Krazy Kat more than 40 years later.

Hooker signed up with Bernie Besman, a record distributor, and his first session produced one of the biggest blues hits ever – 'Boogie Chillen'. It sold more than a million copies. In the next four years, Besman sold Hooker records all over the place (particularly to the Biharis and Specialty), often using different takes of the same song under different titles, to the confusion of collectors. Hooker also recorded for Joe Von Battle, who leased sides to many other labels, including Chess, King, Chance and Savoy.

Many were recorded on primitive equipment, adding to the feeling that they were left over from an earlier era, but Hooker's best work can be found in the hundreds of sides made before 1954. Many of the dance tunes – he repeated the 'Boogie Chillen' theme more often than Elmore James repeated 'Dust My Broom' – include thunderous accompaniment from his own feet, stomping on a footboard just like Blind Lemon Jefferson on 'Hot Dogs' in 1927, or Charley Patton and Skip James. But Hooker's footboard was amplified and sides like 'Rolling Blues' ('Rollin' and Tumblin'' yet again) have an unrivalled, unrestrained, built-in excitement.

In 1955 he moved to the Chicago label Vee-Jay, and his records veered more towards the standard Chicago band style. But it was Vee-Jay that provided his biggest hits like the trite 'Boom Boom' and 'Dimples'. In the early 1960s he cut acoustic albums aimed at the new folk audience, but it was his Vee-Jay sides that influenced new British groups like the Animals and the Rolling Stones.

John Lee Hooker, the 'Boogie Chillen' man and a giant of post-war blues. A brilliant singer and ferocious guitarist and one of the few genuinely unique blues performers.

Dozens more albums followed in various settings, and with accompaniments ranging from Muddy Waters to Canned Heat and Van Morrison. He appeared in films like *The Blues Brothers* (1980) and *The Colour Purple* (1985) after five years of unmemorable recordings, only to find new fame as a guru and elder statesman with a young generation whose parents probably weren't born when he started his long career.

Now in his seventies, Hooker has made albums, like *The Healer* and *Mr Lucky*, with a galaxy of admiring rock stars and younger bluesmen, achieving sales of which he could never have dreamed in the 'Boogie Chillen' days. Yet listen to his singing beneath the glitzy overlays and it is still the same old Hooker, mumbling to himself, introvert, isolated from the music around him.

Hooker and B. B. King are the last really great blues-men from the older generation. King is certainly one of the most important figures of the post-war years, and he

too has been recorded to the point where there seems little new to say. His guitar style owes much to electric jazz guitarist Charlie Christian and T-Bone Walker, and he has made some banal records among the classics, but he is still a powerful live performer and most of his records are worth a listen. He is no relation to Albert King, a powerful singer and distinctive guitarist with a much-copied string-bending action, or Freddy King, a more rock-influenced player, whose raunchy instrumental sides are well worth seeking out.

James Booker (right), an unusually talented singer pianist, who played complex boogies, New Orleans shuffles, ragtime and Chopin in the same set. Sadly under-recorded.

McKies

CHICAGO'S TOP JAZZ SPOT

6323 SOUTH COTTAGE GROVE - - Open till 4 A.M.

OUT TONIGHT?

VISIT
McKIE and CAESAR'S
STEAK HOUSE
6319 South Cottage Grove

Photos

by Mitchell

Look who you might meet at McKies! B B King (left), disc jockey Big Bill Hill and pop star Fontella Bass linger over a drink.

Freddy King (below), one of the great electric guitarists who combined his Texas roots with the new tough sounds of R & B.

7
Today, Today Blues

Into the '90s

As rock and roll grew, so the blues declined. Younger performers like Bobby 'Blue' Bland, Little Junior Parker, Little Milton and even Albert King moved towards soul (a hybrid of rock and gospel) and away from guitar-based backings towards crisper, band-orientated orchestrations. Albert King, who had made some excellent Chicago blues for Parrot in 1953, even joined Stax, a label with an instantly identifiable brass

Bo Diddley in action (main picture), complete with cowboy hat and one of the enormous array of strange-shaped guitars with which he travelled. He made the occasional blues but most of his huge list of recordings were enjoyable R & B novelties.

Little Milton Campbell (left), who recorded for Sun and went on to make a long and successful series of soul-blues records.

Albert King (left), a fine singer guitarist influenced by T-Bone Walker and the unrelated B B King, but much copied by white blues guitarists from Eric Clapton to Johnny Winter.

A real omnibus! This six-wheel giant (above) carried the Albert King band on tour in the sixties and seventies.

riff sound, which specialized in Southern soul singers like Otis Redding and Wilson Pickett. He fitted in well, making some of his best records, such as 'Laundromat Blues' and 'Born Under a Bad Sign', for them.

Freddy King became one of the most important electric guitarists of all, influencing rock, while staying largely within the blues himself. Magic Sam Maghett also showed signs of preparing to cross over before his early death in 1969, and Buddy Guy certainly did in his later, wide-ranging recordings.

Chess managed to get in on the new music with the help of Chuck Berry, a wonderful song-writer and unrivalled chronicler of teenage life, who had a string of big hits across the world, and is still performing to packed houses. Interestingly, many of his B sides were blues.

A label-mate whose jivy, ultra-rhythmic songs also had a blues base was Bo Diddley, another witty and wry song-writer, whose famous shuffle style and spectacular guitar effects were much copied. There was even a British group called the Pretty Things, who took their name from one of his hits. Even the wilder men of rock, like the amazing Little Richard, based a lot of their songs on the blues ('Keep a Knocking' derived from a 1920s' blues by James 'Boodle It' Wiggins), although with few concessions to tradition in arrangements or instrumentation.

Even Muddy Waters and Howlin' Wolf turned to more commercial material, such as 'Got My Mojo Working', 'Mannish Boy' and 'Wang Wang Doodle', but the blues was in a marked decline. Younger blacks felt it was irrevocably linked with a repressive past, the music of

Taj Mahal (below), a clever and eclectic performer capable of turning out superb down-home blues or updating them to suit his mood. He even turned up on a Michelle Shocked album.

Chuck Berry (right), the unrivalled chronicler of teen dreams for more than 40 years. Writer of more rock 'n' roll classics than anyone else and still a powerful performer today.

Joe Hughes (top right) another Texas singer-guitarist in the T-Bone Walker mode. Described by one critic as 'a craftsman but not a master craftsman'.

European blues (above). American John Hammond (left) sings with Hans Theesink from Holland and British bluesman Dave Peabody and harmonica player Rob Mason at Graz in Austria.

Luther 'Snake Boy' Johnson (left) who worked with Elmore James, Otis Spann and Muddy Waters and sang in the Muddy style. He died of cancer in 1976. Not to be confused with Luther 'Guitar Junior' Johnson who, confusingly, also played with Waters.

Blues shouter Nappy Brown (above) who made a long series of jazzy big band blues records for the Savoy label in the forties and fifties.

Big Jay McNeely (below), one of the great honking tenor players of the R & B era, made a successful comeback in the eighties.

Jimmy 'Fast Fingers' Dawkins (above), a fine Chicago blues singer and guitarist, who won the Grand Prix du Disque de Jazz from the Hot Club of France for the best jazz or blues album of 1971.

R & B queen Etta James (below) was popular enough to record hundreds of sides with variable blues interest.

Luther Allison (left) played with the Rolling Stones – a Chicago band, not the British rock group – and with Freddy King and Magic Sam among others. A fine modern bluesman.

Jimmy Witherspoon (above), one of the last of the jazz influenced blues shouters, who has been singing for half a century.

Fenton Robinson (below), a fine Chicago singer and guitarist.

their parents. They had been born in the cities and knew nothing about share-cropping or cotton-picking, and they wanted a music that reflected the noise and speed of urban life. It is no accident that the blues revival was led by white enthusiasts. In 1973 Mike Rowe, the leading British authority on Chicago blues, could already write, tellingly:

The list of obituaries grows ominously longer. Baby Face Leroy is dead, Elmore is dead, J. B. Lenoir was killed in a car crash, Little Walter died in his sleep, apparently after a street brawl; Johnnie Jones died in hospital, as did Otis Spann. Sonny Boy died in Helena, as did Robert Nighthawk. Willie Foster is crippled after a shooting incident, (Jimmy) Reed and Wolf are often sick. Both Earl Hooker and Magic Sam died on the eve of commercial success, an irony particularly reserved for bluesmen.

Since that was written, Howlin' Wolf, Jimmy Reed, Muddy Waters and virtually every member of the first blues generation have all died too. Leonard Chess is also

Jimmy Nelson (above), a fairly minor performer who had one hit with 'T-99'.

The Club Volcano in Jackson (below), Mississippi, a typical southern chitlin circuit club.

Elizabeth Cotten (above), whose 'Freight Train' became an anthem of the skiffle era. She was born in 1892 and made her first records in her sixties.

Son Seals (below), one of the younger Chicago set and a follower of the Albert King style.

gone, his brother Phil disenchanted with the blues world, and after a period of different ownerships and strange leasing deals, their priceless recording archives now belong to the giant MCA.

But the story didn't end there. European interest in blues had been sparked off by visiting artists: Leadbelly in 1948, Big Bill Broonzy in 1951 and Lonnie Johnson in 1952. Brownie McGhee and Sonny Terry turned up in 1958, as did Muddy Waters, who shocked preconceptions with his fierce electric sound. Champion Jack Dupree, a fading figure in New York, found so much British enthusiasm for his music that he settled in Yorkshire.

It was in the early days of the rock era that Lonnie Donegan, banjo player with the Chris Barber Jazz Band, recorded the old Leadbelly song 'Rock Island Line' to fill up a Barber session. It was a surprising major hit, even in

Louisiana-born Lonnie Brooks, also known as Guitar Junior, who recorded widely under that name in the fifties and sixties. A versatile singer-guitarist who never really made a major impact.

Rory Block (above), who, like Bonnie Raitt and Jo-Ann Kelly, consistently and successfully uses the blues as the basis for her own work.

Texan Johnny Copeland (below), a tough R & B singer guitarist who recorded for a variety of labels, including one album cut on the Ivory Coast with African horns and percussion.

the USA, and spawned numerous groups playing in the skiffle style of the old black washboard bands. One of the best records was 'Freight Train', picked up by folk singer Peggy Seeger from her black housemaid, Elizabeth Cotten, and sung to great effect by Nancy Whiskey. Cotten's own, gentler version was recorded by Folkways in 1958, when she was 66.

The blues influence in rock had been noticed, especially in records by Fats Domino, Ray Charles, Chuck Berry, Bo Diddley, Little Richard and even Elvis Presley, one of the few white singers whose versions of black songs were not just pale imitations. White Southerners, such as Carl Perkins and Jerry Lee Lewis, also performed blues, like Blind Lemon's 'Matchbox Blues', in their repertoire, as did Eddie Cochran (Kokomo Arnold's 'Milk Cow Blues') and the Rooftop Singers (Gus Cannon's 'Walk

Snooks Eaglin (left), who managed to record down-home country blues and tough R & B sides for different labels at the same time. After years of neglect, he is now more popular than ever with a new updated sound.

Louisiana Red (below), also known as Rockin' Red, Cryin' Red, Playboy Fuller, Rocky Fuller, and even Elmore James Jnr, but who is more successful in Europe than at home.

Bowling Green John Cephas and Phil Wiggins (above) from Washington DC who recreate the melodic East Coast sound of Sonny Terry and Brownie McGhee.

Sam Lightnin' Hopkins (right), who got his nickname after teaming up with pianist Wilson 'Thunder' Smith. He was a brilliant singer and guitarist and a wonderful improviser.

Right In'). This black-white interchange was more common than realized in rural areas in the 1920s and 1930s; white singers like Jimmy Rodgers, Frank Hutchinson, the Allen Brothers and Jimmie Davis sang blues or recorded with black musicians, and the Mississippi Sheiks, Andrew and Jim Baxter, Willie McTell and the Memphis jug bands all included white material. It was a shared tradition, demonstrated in the early 1950s by Presley's interest in black songs.

In the USA the young Bob Dylan followed his mentor, Woody Guthrie, in singing blues such as 'See That My Grave Is Kept Clean' (Lemon Jefferson), 'Fixin' to Die' (Bukka White), 'Jesus Gonna Make up My Dyin' Bed' (Blind Willie Johnson) or 'Highway 51' (Tommy McClennan). There was a growing interest in the blues, and a new curiosity.

A variety of white enthusiasts – American and European – began making field trips, like the record companies of old, and discovered many fine acts never before recorded. Frederick Ramsey found Cat Iron, a grim old Mississippi singer with a compelling, archaic style, and Scott Dunbar, while Sam Charters traced survivors of the Memphis jug bands and relaunched Lightnin' Hopkins, then in decline, on a new career.

In Louisiana Harry Oster and Richard Allen taped major artists such as Robert Pete Williams and Snooks Eaglin (now a highly popular performer in a new, updated style), while Alan Lomax and British folk singer Shirley Collins toured the South in 1959, discovering Forest City Joe, who had previously recorded unsuccessfully for Chess, John Dudley, who gave them a magnificent slide version of 'Poor Boy', and, most importantly, Fred McDowell.

McDowell was an outstanding singer and slide guitar player, discovered at his peak, whose breathtaking playing suggested that the 1930s and 1940s had never happened. He toured and recorded widely and effectively, and is probably the last of the truly great Mississippi country bluesmen.

There were discoveries in the cities, too. French enthusiast Jacques Demetre obtained the sole known interview wth Kokomo Arnold, and took some of the very few photographs of Elmore James. Paul Oliver, Chris Strachwitz, Mack McCormick, John Fahey, Gayle Dean Wardlow, Nick Perls, Dick Waterman, Bruce Bastin and a handful of other researchers used clues on records and from interviewing elderly blacks, and found veterans from the early days of the blues: Son House,

Lefty Dizz (above), Mr Hi-Energy. Once a member of Hound Dog Taylor's Houserockers and something of a clown on stage.

Tough down-home bluesman George 'Wild Child' Butler (below) who played with Sonny Boy Williamson, Junior Wells and Lightnin' Hopkins but who never really made it big himself.

Boogie Woogie Red (Vernon Harrison) (left), a Detroit singer and piano player who recorded with Baby Boy Warren and John Lee Hooker in the fifties, and later made some under-rated albums of his own.

Frank Frost (right) from Mississippi whose wonderful small band sides for Sam Phillips in 1962 are eagerly sought by collectors.

Walter 'Wolfman' Washington (below) from New Orleans played with Lee Dorsey and Irma Thomas before making some undistinguished records of his own.

Bukka White and Skip James, three of the greatest Mississippi singers; Furry Lewis, Robert Wilkins, Gus Cannon, Will Shade and Bo Carter in Memphis; Black Ace in Texas; Peg Leg Howell in Atlanta; Sleepy John Estes in Tennessee.

John Hurt was traced to Avalon, the town he sang about on his 1928 session, Rube Lacey and Ishmon Bracey had become preachers, while Joe Callicott was farming. There were many more, too, of varying merit and obscurity. Some were recorded and had brief new careers as concert artists, even visiting Europe in a series of American Folk Blues Festivals throughout the 1960s. Others, like Howell, Carter and Memphis Minnie were too far gone in sickness or poverty to participate, but took some comfort from knowing they had not been entirely forgotten.

The original 78s by the old performers had been collected by a small circle of enthusiasts, upon whose collections all subsequent reissues have been based. Some are incredibly rare, with only one or two copies known, but the new reissue labels have let them be heard by more people than the originals ever were.

The most influential reissue was a six-LP set, *Anthology of American Music*, compiled by Harry Smith

Virginian John Jackson (above) had a comprehensive repertoire of East Coast blues and dances and white country material. A distinctive singer and fine guitarist.

Big Joe Duskin (below), a lesser known pianist, who has delighted audiences on his European tours.

Katie Webster (above), house pianist for Excello records for many years and a fine boogie pianist and singer.

Johnny Winter (below), an albino singer-guitarist of considerable skills. He revived Muddy Waters' flagging career with a fine series of albums on Blue Sky Records.

for Folkways, and which included every kind of music from jazz and Cajun to blues and gospel. However, the Origin Jazz Library, Arhoolie and Yazoo labels in the USA and the Roots and Document labels in Austria have done most to alert a new generation to the wealth of old blues music. There were many other enthusiast labels in the 1960s – Matchbox, Down With the Game, Highway 51 and Flyright were the best. The big companies, who officially owned the copyrights, made a few desultory efforts at reissues, but their best efforts have been in the CD era – ironically, often after their copyrights have expired.

The blues revival spread to performances, too. Numerous young blues listeners first learned about the music from the Rolling Stones, who played songs by Robert Johnson, Howlin' Wolf, Robert Wilkins and Chuck Berry and from other blues-based groups such as the Animals, the Pretty Things and the Groundhogs, and performers like Alexis Korner, Cyril Davis, Ian Anderson, Eric Clapton, Jeremy Spencer, Dave Peabody and Jo Ann Kelly. Some, like Spencer, did little more than repeat the sound of the originals; others, like Clapton, used the blues as a base on which to build their own ideas.

In the USA there were many performers with blues in their repertoire: Paul Butterfield, the Grateful Dead, Jefferson Airplane, Johnny Winter and Canned Heat (named after a Tommy Johnson song). In recent years there has been a big growth in white blues bands, such as Stevie Ray Vaughan and the Fabulous Thunderbirds, and George Thorogood and the Destroyers.

The blues boom faded away with overkill, but the dreariness of the pop scene in the 1980s led to renewed interest, largely fuelled by mainstream enthusiasm for Robert Cray. The introduction of the CD, with its extra fidelity and increased playing time, sparked off a new recording and reissue frenzy, too, and virtually every great blues record from the past is now easily available. Blues are even used to sell lager, jeans and cold remedies on TV and radio.

What of the performers? A new breed of bluesman has arisen, adding elements of soul, gospel and rock to the music – another irony, as all three elements themselves derived partly from blues. The most successful is Cray, a superb guitarist whose songs have melodic strength, structured power and contemporary relevance. There is much of the Stax sound in his arrangements, but he is truly a bluesman for the 1990s, who appeals to a much wider audience than blues buyers.

The other most promising name is Joe Louis Walker

Robert Cray (above), who reawakened general interest in the blues in the late eighties with a brilliant series of soul-blues fusion records.

Paul Butterfield (right), a highly regarded musician among white blues fans, gets cooking with squeezebox giant Clifton Chenier.

Alexis Korner (above), most influential of early British blues singers, whose records inspired the Rolling Stones among others. His radio shows were required listening for budding blues fans who knew little about the music.

Magic Slim (below), leader of The Teardrops, and a guardian of the Chicago style.

The generation game (left). Backstage at the Handy Blues Awards show in Memphis are (from left), Hubert Sumlin, Rufus Thomas, Stevie Ray Vaughan, Robert Cray and Albert King.

Eric Clapton (above), who took the blues and added his own individual stamp. A creator rather than a simple copyist like so many others.

Joe Louis Walker (below), a marvellous West Coast singer-guitarist and one of the best of the new breed of blues singers willing to expand the traditional framework without veering totally into rock. A mesmeric live performer.

Albert Collins (above), another
hero of the white blues bands.
A cousin of Lightnin' Hopkins,
he is generally regarded as
the finest of the younger
Texan guitarists.

Carey Bell (below), a Chicago
club musician who played
with Eddie Taylor, Earl
Hooker, John Lee Hooker,
Muddy Waters and others.
Father of young blues lumi-
nary Lurrie Bell.

Charlie Musselwhite, a
white harmonica player
who has played with some
of the best black musicians.

The Kinsey Report, a highly
regarded family-based rock
group with solid blues roots.

from the West Coast, a striking singer and excellent guitarist, who again fuses other elements of modern music into his blues.

Other notables include Lil' Ed and the Blues Imperials, a steaming, mixed-race band, like so many of the new wave, Kenny Neal from Louisiana, the Kinsey Report, Anson Funderburgh, Phillip Walker and Lurrie Bell, among many, many more, who are offering an updated version of the music.

Despite the growing number of new artists, Red Lick, Britain's biggest blues mail-order company, says its biggest sellers remain the Chess stars, especially with the trend towards boxed set reissues of their complete works. (The complete Chess recordings of Muddy Waters was Red Lick's biggest hit of the year.) Hound Dog Taylor, an Elmore James disciple, is another in constant demand, as is J. B. Hutto, one of the hardest of all Chicago singers.

With further irony, more and more people are turning to white performers – both solo and with bands – who tend to create the sounds of an earlier era, while black performers like Cray and Walker move forwards.

Blues may be close on a century old, it may be a limited form of musical expression, but there's plenty more life left in what has been described as the Western world's last great folk music.

B B King and Lucille (top above), his equally famous guitar, have taken the blues all over the world. Two of the all time greats.

Phillip Walker (above), who worked with Rosco Gordon and Lonesome Sundown before joining zydeco giant Clifton Chenier. Better known as a versatile sideman for numerous R & B singers from Lowell Fulson and Jimmy Reed to Little Richard and Fats Domino, although he has made some good records of his own.

Junior Wells and Buddy Guy, one of the great blues partnerships of the seventies (left).

Further Reading

A selective bibliography

Anyone interested in reading more about the blues will find the following books among the best and most trustworthy guides to the music.

Black Gospel, Viv Broughton (Blandford Press, London, 1985)
Attractive history of the blues' Sunday cousin.

Blacks, Whites and Blues, Tony Russell (Studio Vista, London, 1970)
First-rate analysis of the relationship between black and white folk music.

The Blackwell Guide to Blues Records, ed. Paul Oliver (Blackwell, Oxford, 1989)
Generally trustworthy guide to blues reissues; paperback reprint includes more CDs.

Blues and Gospel Records 1902–1943, R. M. W. Dixon and J. Godrich, (Storyville Publications, revised 3rd edition, Essex, 1982)
A detailed discography of every pre-war blues and gospel record.

Blues Fell This Morning, Paul Oliver (Cambridge University Press, Cambridge, revised edition, 1990)
The classic study of the meaning of the blues.

The Bluesmakers, Samuel Charters (Da Capo Press, New York, 1991)
Revised reprint of two early books by one of the best blues writers of all.

Blues Off the Record, Paul Oliver (Baton Press, 1984)
Thirty years of blues commentary by Britain's most evocative blues writer.

Blues Records 1943–1970: A to K, Mike Leadbitter and Neil Slaven (Record Information Services, London, 1987)
First of two projected volumes covering the post-war years.

Blues Who's Who, Sheldon Harris (Da Capo Press, New York, 1987)
A 775-page biography of virtually every major blues singer.

Chicago Blues, Mike Rowe (Da Capo Press, New York, 1981)
Originally written in 1973, but still the best survey of the rich Chicago blues tradition.

Deep South Piano, Karl Gert zur Heide (Studio Vista, London, 1970)
Virtually all that is known about the great piano players.

The Devil's Music, Giles Oakley (Ariel Books, London, revised edition, 1983)
Very informative history of the music, based on BBC documentaries.

Down Home Guide to the Blues, Frank Scott (A Cappella Books, Chicago, 1991)
Enthusiastic guide to worldwide blues reissues, largely on LP.

Good Rockin' Tonight, Colin Escott with Martin Hawkins (Virgin Books, London, 1992)
Detailed study of the important Sun label.

King of the Delta Blues, Stephen Calt and Gayle Dean Wardlow (Rock Chapel Press, New Jersey, 1988)
Comprehensive study of Charley Patton and the early Deep South blues.

Ma Rainey and the Classic Blues Singers, Derrick Stewart-Baxter (Studio Vista, London, 1970)
One of the best studies of the early women stars.

Memphis Blues, Bengt Olsson (Studio Vista, London, 1970)
A Look at one of the most important blues cities.

Blues on Record

Red River Blues, Bruce Bastin (University of Illinois Press, Chicago, 1986)
Unrivalled study of the music and the singers in the southeastern states.

Savannah Syncopators, Paul Oliver (Studio Vista, London, 1970)
A look at African influences in the blues.

Searching for Robert Johnson, Peter Guralnick (Secker & Warburg, London, 1990)
Stop-gap biography of the great man.

The Sound of the City, Charlie Gillett (Souvenir Press, London, revised edition, 1983)
Rhythm and blues to rock and roll.

South to Louisiana, John Broven (Pelican Books, Louisiana, 1987)
Cajun, zydeco, blues and swamp pop.

The Story of the Blues, Paul Oliver (Barrie & Rockcliff, London, 1969)
Profusely illustrated history of the singers and the music.

Woman With Guitar – Memphis Minnie's Blues, Paul and Beth Garon (Da Capo Press, New York, 1992)
The best blues biography yet of the most important female blues singer of all.

The CD era has seen a tremendous increase in blues reissues, and virtually every major blues singer is either available on CD or planned to be. European reissues tend to be better value with more tracks because copyright laws in the USA make long-playing CDs too expensive.

The biggest pre-war reissue company is Document and its subsidiaries in Austria, run by veteran collector Johnny Parth, who intends to preserve *every* available blues on CD. There are more than 200 CDs available so far, with many more planned.

In England the Interstate group has the Flyright, Travelin' Man, Krazy Kat and Magpie labels, covering both pre- and post-war blues reissues, and there are some fine albums on JSP.

The major American reissue label for early blues is Yazoo, whose catalogue is largely duplicated by Document. Both Sony–CBS and RCA have their own reissue series.

There are many more post-war labels, some devoted to reissues and others to new recordings. In England Ace has a huge reissue programme drawn from some of the best of the small post-war labels, such as Modern, Flair, Dig and Specialty. Charly and MCA are digging into the Chess catalogue to great effect, and Charly also has numerous Vee-Jay and Sun reissues. The German Bear Family has some superb, brilliantly documented albums and boxed sets from Sun and other post-war labels. In the USA the labels Arhoolie, Relic, Trumpet, Prestige, Stax, Atlantic and the Rounder Group can always be trusted.

New recordings of the highest quality can be found on such labels as Antones, Alligator, Black Top, Bullseye and Demon.

Very few record shops stock more than a handful of blues labels outside London, so most buyers have to depend on mail order. The biggest and best blues mail-order company is Red Lick Records, PO Box 3, Porthmadog, Gwynedd LL48 6AQ, which also publishes regular catalogues of thousands of blues albums from Europe and the USA.

Index

Groveton High School Library
38 State St.
Groveton, NH 03582